from misery to happiness

How to Become **Authentically** Happy
and
Make the World a **Happier** Place

Go Shining!

Carolyn [illegible]

from misery to happiness

How to Become **Authentically** Happy
and
Make the World a **Happier** Place

Carolyn Berry

www.carolynberry.com

1. Happiness — Self-help —Recovery — Inspirational — Psychological Aspects — Transformational

ISBN # 978-0-9964555-0-3

Edited by Marj Pendergraft

Cover / Interior Design by Jacqueline Mallegni

www.carolynberry.com

Published By

To my daughter, Colleen Nufer and son, Johnny Berry, who survived my misery; and then went on to support my recovery, to love me unconditionally, and to celebrate my journey into authentic happiness.

Acknowledgments

My heartfelt gratitude goes out to the following creative and skillful women whom I depended on through this book's birthing: Marj Pendergraft, the midwife of this "labor of love," who was there from the beginning, patiently encouraging, supporting and challenging me to bring it into this world. And when the initial draft was completed, Marj tirelessly put in long hours to clean it up with her astute editing skills. Jacqueline Mallegni, a renaissance woman, took the pages of this book and gave them a structural design and then created a cover that shines. Robin Quinn, a long-time LA editor and book coach, rounded out the team, giving the book a final review and providing valuable feedback.

A special thanks goes out to all my teachers along the way: The people in the rooms of my recovery program who helped me to open my heart, to practice acceptance and gratitude, and to believe in a Higher Power; and the wise ones-Dr. Janice Kalec, Berenice Glass, LCSW, Grandfathers Wallace Black Elk and Morning Owl, Medicine Woman Lily Teresa, my mother, my children, my grandchildren, my sister, my grandparents, my friends, my ancestors, the Great Spirit and all of her/his creations-Grandfather Sun, Grandmother Moon, Mother Earth and her mountains, the waters, the deserts, the valleys, and all my relations.

And I am forever grateful to the following extraordinary cheerleaders...my "sisters" and "brother" who each gave their particular brand of support and valuable suggestions that helped polish this book: Orolyn "Goldie" Benson, LPN, Terri Blake, Brion Clarkson, Russell Evans, Dr. Janice Kalec, Judy Molnar, Colleen Nufer, Kathleen Radcliffe, and Sierra Sanchez, MFT. Their influence made it possible for me to grow to believe that I have insights worth writing down and sharing.

My father who, left this Earth in 1987, taught me that I could do anything I chose to–even write a book; Dorothea Patrick, who showed me the value of honesty and loved me back into this world before she left it; and Richie and Roz Annenberg who have inspired me for over 25 years.

You are all the best...Go Shining!

CONTENTS

Size matters not. Look at me. Judge me by my size, do you? Hmm? Hmm.

And well you should not. For my ally is the Force, and a powerful ally it is. Life creates it, makes it grow. Its energy surrounds us and binds us. Luminous beings are we, not this crude matter.

You must feel the Force around you; here, between you, me, the tree, the rock, everywhere, yes.

—Yoda

INTRODUCTION

Look to This Day

Listen to the exhortation of the dawn!
Look to this day, For it is life, the very life of life.
In its brief course lie all the
Verities and realities of your existence.
The bliss of growth, The glory of action,
The splendor of beauty;
For yesterday is but a dream,
And to-morrow is only a vision;
But to-day well lived makes
Every yesterday a dream of happiness,
And every tomorrow a vision of hope.
Look well, therefore, to this day.
Such is the salutation of the dawn!

— Kalidasa

When I started thinking about writing a book about my happiness, I realized that happiness means different things to different people. Since I am most familiar with my own experiences about happiness, I will be expounding on what it means to me. I am not talking about the kind of happiness you feel when you get a new boyfriend or girlfriend; or purchase a new car or home; or get a raise or promotion at the job; or win the "big" game. The happiness I am referring to is the kind of happiness that is generated from the inside. It is found deep within the core of our being; it is a basic part of our nature - and it can be developed by enhancing particular attitudes. Throughout the following pages I will be calling it, interchangeably, "intrinsic" or "authentic" happiness.

What I am sharing with you is how intrinsic happiness grew within me. When I look back I know I was not looking for happiness; first I was on a quest for freedom from depression and mental anguish and when I completed that quest, a door opened to another one. I entered through that door into a quest for a better way of life - and that led me to a quest for a better me. Through practicing the virtues that became part of my daily life, I became truly happy. These are the virtuous qualities I primarily and most consistently actuate in my life - the four virtues that I discovered always precede and then nurture my state of happiness:

Acceptance, Gratitude, Constructive Attention, Love

To grow my happiness I tend to feed each virtue with as much conscious devotion as my human imperfection allows at given periods in my life. I just do the best I can, continuing to "weed, feed and cultivate" these qualities so they grow strong, proliferate, and sustain an intrinsically happy life.

I experience Acceptance, Gratitude, Constructive Attention, and Love as working together. They interrelate and connect through a common looping system that is powered by Spirit - which I also refer to as our energy or life force - that functions as part of the intricate, dynamic paradigm of universal inter-connectedness. You may notice that when I am writing about my experience with any of the four virtues there will usually be one or more of the others involved.

For example, when I grasp that I am being sabotaged by a shortcoming like false-pride and admit to myself that it is hindering me, I am Grateful that I recognize it and can Accept it as a something I myself am enacting so that I can begin to change it and get to the other side of it. I am paying *Constructive Attention to it as an unwelcome trait that I choose to free myself from so that I can move forward. I do not beat myself up about it like I used to do; that is inevitably related to my bogus thoughts of myself

**Constructive Attention is my description of focusing positive attention to what we want to grow in our lives.*

as some kind of despicable character that resulted in persistent self-destructive attention.

The four virtues open an infinite number of doors to other virtues. Acceptance opens the door for Love to be received and given. I walk through another door and I am full of Gratitude for all the Love that I receive and give. The door to paying Constructive Attention opened up and shed a light that grows my Acceptance, Love and Gratitude. And the doors of Acceptance, Love and Gratitude take me to where and how I pay attention. So it is that if only one of these virtues is cultivated, cross-pollination will begin.

Acceptance opens the door to Peace.
Gratitude opens the door to Enthusiasm.
Attention opens the door to Self-Esteem.
Love opens the door to Inter-connectedness.
Weave them together and voila! -
Authentic Happiness!

I Love all of life. I Love my life!

As you see, the practice of growing these virtues not only enhances my humanity, it transforms me into a human being that primarily flows along in a radiance of positive energy - what I refer to as my Spirit, my Energy, or my Life Force.

This little book with a big smile is my way of sharing the stumbling trek I made that took me on a trail through a valley of misery to what a majority of people say they want most-Happiness.

By relating my lessons on the rambling road I stumbled along as I moved into an essentially happy life, it is my intention to make your trek to happiness an easier and more direct one. I attempt to clearly mark the paths I have navigated for the past 30-plus years. Hopefully you can spread your own message of happiness sooner than I did. From most journeys, stories emerge. Some of my stories exemplify what and how I learned about living along the way to my happiness. Including ALL of my challenges, mishaps, and victories would have become burdensome for me and probably for you...so I just picked a few I thought most relevant.

I have inserted some exercises that I have practiced and invite you to use, or not, and have set aside some spaces on the pages for them. If you do not choose to use them as suggested, you can make notes, doodle, or put your own imaginations into the spaces - they are held for your own use.

My life today is about bringing happiness to all of my experiences and not making any into a burden. I used to do that, you know. Now I consciously strive to do the opposite, making what some would label burdens into enjoyable endeavors. Usually it works. I do not believe the road I travel is the only way. I believe there are infinite paths to intrinsic happiness.

I hope you discover the way that calls to you and that you embrace it passionately.

If sharing my journey resonates with you or spills light upon your path, it will add to the satisfaction I have already received. If this book helps even one person onto a road to intrinsic happiness it has done its job.

> *Thousands of candles can be lighted from a single candle, and the life of the candle will not be shortened. Happiness never decreases by being shared.*
>
> — Buddha

Go Shining!

An Invitation Each day look in the mirror and smile at yourself until you see your eyes smile. An honest smile is one of the doorways to inner happiness.

A Suggestion You may enjoy reading this book by turning to random pages instead of reading it straight through. I encourage you to read some of it while you are out in nature. That is where most of it was conceived.

A Note "Go Shining" is a salutation I adopted from Grandma Evelyn Eaton (December 22, 1902-July 17, 1983) who did ceremony regularly in Lone Pine, California. After ceremony she would tell each participant as they were leaving, "Go Shining! You are a warrior of the light." Dr. Janice Kalec, a dear friend and teacher, told me this story. It resonated with me and I have now used it as my salutation for over 20 years. I am told she doesn't mind.

Chapter One

. . . .

THE BEGINNING

Life is a series of natural and spontaneous changes. Don't resist them - that only creates sorrow. Let reality be reality. Let things flow naturally forward in whatever way they like.

— Lao Tzu

When I was growing up, acting happy was required by my parents and other family members. Smiling translated into "Everything is okay," not into "I am a really happy person." A smile-less face attracted questions like: "What's wrong with you?"... "Is something the matter?..."Did something happen at school today?"... "Why are you down in the dumps?"..."What do you have to be so unhappy about?"...And the one that grated on me the very most: "If you aren't careful you're going to trip over your lower lip."

But one upside to this family pattern was that smiling did make me feel a level of happiness. It just wasn't the kind that went deep; it was more like a veneer. It was shiny but not the real thing.

Another upside was (and is) that my lips curve into smiles with natural ease! Yet, for the first 30-some odd years of my life my smile was a habit more than a genuine expression of joy. Even though sometimes it was connected to a happy feeling, most of the time I didn't know when it was and when it wasn't. It was part of an unconscious façade that I created to meet my family's requirements - and that façade became my pseudo-identity. I realize now that, like many people, I didn't really know what happiness is. All I knew was that I smiled to tell my world that I was okay - and I thought I was okay but I was fooling us both! My smile was just one part of my long journey on the road of attempting to be what I thought everyone wanted me to be. Eventually, this posturing provoked my entrance into an insidious maze that drew me in deeper and deeper... until I was lost. And losing one's Self, as some of you may know, can take you right into the Valley of Despair - a valley where everything grows into a dark, disturbing snarl that propagates even darker disturbing snarls. Down and down I went in an unending spiral of anxiety, which I soothed and rearranged with scotch and gin and other handy *intoxicators.*

After too many long, hard years of continuing this painful, alcohol-induced downward spiral into misery, I woke up to the recurrent incongruence between my smiling face and the mounting sadness and distress storming around inside of me - and I felt like a phony much of the time. I believed that I was conning everyone in my life with a smile that wasn't connected to my heart or any other part of me. I desperately longed to find the ME I had lost. My misery was torturing me. All I wanted to do was to feel better.

There was a miniscule amount of positive "something" going on intermittently inside of me that sprinkled some light across this dark, lonely life that I wanted to escape. I began searching in books, writing meager, morose poetry, analyzing movie characters, listening to people's stories. In each of these I looked for parts of myself. But being blind to all my options, I figured that I needed to escape from the relentless ache by drinking myself into oblivion.

The unsurprising result was that I was cited for two DUIs within a three month period and was mandated to enter a driver's diversion program that led me to a Recovery Program. Paradoxically, it was my out-of-control drinking that opened the door to a new and beneficial way of life - one that offered peace of mind, freedom from unbearable emotional pain, and the virtues that lead to true happiness.

I now became involved in a Program where I experienced one of the things I had lost...a feeling of belonging...being connected. The principles of this Program worked for me because I was willing to do whatever it took to get release from my pain and fear - even to follow directions that made no sense to me. At this point, I was convinced that someone - or likely almost everyone - knew more about living than I did. Actually, this was one of the few beliefs I had that vaguely smacked of some kind of connection to reality. Although I fought it tooth and nail, I eventually acknowledged that my thinking had become horribly distorted - and so I became increasingly willing to ask for opinions and clarifications from people I respected, until at last my own thinking was on solid ground.

I learned to be there for others when they reached out for my help, as I learned the importance of reaching out for help when I needed it. However, to this day I am challenged by the process of recognizing when I do need it; I learned that I have a tendency to think that unless I am in a life-threatening situation, I can handle my problems myself. I pay a ridiculous price for this false-pride attitude and I look forward to the day that I overcome it more routinely. I have come to understand that I needed to make a real, honest commitment to my conscious growth, and forevermore to strive for progress towards being a healthier "spiritual being." Of course, it took time... months and even years...for me to see progress in some areas of my life. And now I know that journey is never over - progress, by its very meaning, implies continuous forward movement.

In the Recovery Program I learned about examining the inside of myself, identifying my responsibilities to me and to others, growing to accept me, and connecting to a Higher Power. I was starting to move out of the Valley of Despair into a place where I could see the world in a clearer and brighter light. During this resurrection period I was urged along through several fluctuating, transitional years of self-exploration.

I discovered that the unhealthy part of me found comfort in the old, familiar ways and wanted to stay true to the patterns that were woven into my former miserable life. That part of me kept tending to sabotage my attempts to change. It was a relief to experience those old patterns growing weaker over time.

I have received innumerable lessons reminding me that if I get complacent and begin to back-pedal, my unhealthy parts that survive will grow strong again - and possibly bring new unhealthy patterns along with them. It is my job to focus on and grow the healthy parts of me, the parts I want to thrive and be strong.

I am grateful that during the early stages of my journey, motivated by the desire to be free of that awful pain, I was able to keep my focus primarily on my healthy parts and remain true to my commitment to progress. I was driven to make the necessary changes NO MATTER WHAT. That meant that I used all my resources to stay conscious of reality, of my true values, in all parts of my life. So my healthy parts did become much stronger - and now they compose the perennial garden of my life! This I credit to me picking up and using the tools introduced to me by the Recovery Program that showed me how to plant seeds of honesty, gratitude, love and service in my Self and to follow the principles that provide enhanced meaning to my life.

Throughout the years I opened up to many invaluable specific instances of help that came to me from a variety of guiding forces, starting with the Principles of the Program of Recovery and the people in the rooms who knew how to apply them in their own lives. And then like train cars, I added to them an endless ensemble of sources to help me pursue my own evolution: I received important insights from some psychotherapy and enhanced my learning by engaging in higher education; I earned a BS degree in Human Services and an MA Degree in Marriage and Family Therapy (It took me 20 years to get these degrees; I think my shortcomings interfered quite a few times!); I have been blessed through the years with some great friends pursuing their own spiritual growth who have been models and inspired me along my path; then there have been the wise elders and children who have shared their teachings; additionally, I have been affected by reading provocative inspirational books, many of which were written as children's books; and finally, there have been my greatest teachers of all, that are everywhere, all around me...the trees, stones, winged-ones, four-legged-ones, creepy-crawlies, ones-with-no-legs, water-ones, and the water, fire, winds, stars, sun and moon.

With the guidance of these generous, steadfast forces, I have grown... slowly, steadily... and in spite of my endless devices for interrupting my progress... and over time I have developed a meaningful relationship with my Higher Power which I call Great Spirit, the Great Mystery or The Creator.

So I have evolved, becoming a positive individual - and a Soul connected-directed happy human being with a truly authentic shining smile, who knows most of the mistakes that can be made on the way to bliss!

I don't think we can have too many teachers or guides throughout our lifetimes!

> *Let my soul smile through my heart and my heart smile through my eyes, that I may scatter rich smiles in sad hearts.*
>
> — Paramahansa Yogananda

During my journey I have awakened to the idea that being happy is not only about enjoying life, it is about sharing our joy with our family, community and world. After all - earlier I had certainly shared my misery! To make this significant life change I learned I must amend my inner world - my thinking, my feelings and my perceptions. I believe that we each are the nuts and bolts of the "infrastructure" of our social systems, so to make profound changes to our society's adverse paradigms we must first change ourselves.

Here's a thought for self-empowerment...When you change any aspect of your own life, you change an aspect of the world!

I believe in efforts to heal the world. It seems pretty apparent that civilizations have drifted from a Spirit-Centered to a Financial-Centered paradigm in searching for better societies that help those in need and/or in poverty - and ironically, have instead created a world driven by greed and fear that fosters widespread compliance with mundane values and depression.

Presently, as a universal response to this skewed configuration, teachers are coming from all directions and diverse backgrounds with a united message that says something like this:

It is time to shift. It is time to regain our equilibrium, harmony and love of life by reinstating an authentic faith in a Great Universal Creator and in the inter-connectedness of all life. We must replace the faulty faith we have been putting in ideologies and dogmatic doctrines that promote division, conflict, intolerance and imbalance. It is time to grow our courage instead of our fear; our love instead of our hate; our generosity instead of our greed; our creativity instead of our routineness; our happiness instead of our depression. It is time for us to restructure our paradigm of civilization to one that is Spirit-Centered, putting economics back in its place as one single aspect of the priorities that reflect how we construct the Circle of our Life.

A happy, generous society is a cooperative, compassionate society that can create not only prosperous individuals but a prosperous society, driven by Life-Force...Spirit. Instead of community values built upon financial concerns, it is time for us to build our community values upon a Spirit-centered paradigm grown out of the soil of happiness. I believe that together we can make this shift in our society - one person at a time. I believe that every time one of us becomes authentically happy we inspire another to become authentically happy. Then families grow happier, and neighborhoods do too, and eventually happiness is intertwined into the social fiber of our communities and our society. According to scientific studies, "happiness is contagious."

I have experienced this phenomenon of "happiness contagion." For two years I have been visiting family and friends all across the country, consciously sharing my happiness. I have been told by some that they have felt happier since spending time with me. Chances are that in turn they will pass forward some of that happiness to those that cross their paths.

From Misery to Happiness shares the realizations and the knowledge that I have acquired during my 30-plus years of personal evolution. It is my hope that this book will do its small part in helping to shift our world back into balance by each one of us growing happiness in our souls that we in turn spread into our families' and friends' homes and communities. To me being an intrinsically happy person means that bliss permeates all parts of the person's inner and outer worlds, lighting the way to thrive in solitude and in togetherness; to move through the dark into the light; to create solutions bred from problems; to transform fear into a fleeting feature, inviting faith to sprout like a clinging vine does from robust roots. It is about living with that happy feeling in our gut 80+ percent of the time, leaving that other 20-percent to remind us that we are not perfect and it is incumbent upon us to stay awake to what and how we want to grow.

Since I have experienced the welcome contagion of happiness, I consider it a privilege to be able to take part in the spreading of it. As we pass it on we change our world, as it has always been changed - a little bit at a time. *From Misery to Happiness* invites you to become a contributor to the creation of a happier world...a smile at a time.

Chapter Two

. . . .

HAPPINESS

Happiness is intrinsic. It's an internal thing. When you build it into yourself, no external circumstances can take it away.

— (Unknown)

Exploring What Happiness Is and Isn't

It is not easy to find happiness in ourselves,
and it is not possible to find it elsewhere.

— Agnes Repplier,

I do not see happiness as a simple feeling. I believe it is a growing state of being.

I often wonder what our world would be like if "happiness loves company" was as common an aphorism as "misery loves company."

After endless attempts to get happiness from outside of myself, I finally came to understand that a person's sustainable core happiness cannot be given to and received from someone or something. If you have tried to "make" someone happy or to get it for yourself from "out there" somewhere, you may have experienced a moment where you thought you had accomplished it, but it was like catching a cloud; it didn't last, and soon changed or evaporated.

Externally produced happiness is pleasure-based, whether we give it or receive it. That kind of happy feeling is meant to slip into our sweet memories where it can be remembered and re-experienced. But it is only a transitory feeling that we'd like to hold on to or have more of the time, and can't.

From the lessons of my personal journey and the stories I have heard from others over a period of nearly four decades as a professional counselor and Life Coach, I have come to believe that we all have specific positive characteristics that feed the soul, that can seed and cultivate a deep-rooted genuine condition of happiness.

I entered the threshold to a blessed bliss by consciously agreeing to undertake a challenging evolutionary journey into becoming a grateful, accepting, loving, attentive, spirit-incited being. For me the road to intrinsic happiness has been an arduous journey, full of wrong turns and waylaying events.

I have a tendency to get complacent or sidetracked or both, which helps me to avoid full-blown, focused consciousness by lulling me into dull-mindedness. I also learned it is hard for me to work toward something when I am not clear on what that something is. After all, I wasn't aware that what I wanted was to "grow" intrinsic happiness within me. I was just looking for a heartfelt smile and a life that felt better than the one I was struggling to live. So I moved like a meandering river of muck through my evolutionary happiness junket.

Upon reviewing my journey to authentic happiness, I now realize that I had often been misguided and frequently had misinterpreted the "what" and "how" of happiness - as depicted by my parents, friends, books, magazines, movies, television, advertisements, and even some self-help pundits.

The basic message I took in is that happiness is found outside myself, in people, places and things: by being loved; by having a good job; by having a busy social life; by taking a two week vacation every year; by driving the "right" car; by residing in the "right" zip code; by being part of a popular "right" group of friends; by wearing stylish clothing; and by having lots of purchasing power. And, to some degree I practiced them all!

I remember...

When I was a little kid I felt happy when my mom and dad were pleased by something I did and when other kids wanted to play with me.

My long-time friend, Judy, reminded me that when I was a teenager my happiness was dependent on me being part of the in-group, going "steady," or having a date or a party to go to, and definitely having something to do every weekend - that is, being popular enough to be included in social activities and special events.

In my late teens being happy was about being in long-term committed relationships, getting engaged and then getting married...

Theme:
Happiness is based on being wanted...loved!

When I was 20, I married. And at that time, even though I experienced being in a loving marriage, it couldn't sustain my happiness - something was still missing. So in my early 20's I had two beautiful children. Most of my pregnancy was bliss...I got tons of attention. I was a young mommy; I had a daughter and a son; I had a lovely, model family of four. Now I was sure I would be happy forever. I had everything a woman could want: A doting, handsome husband, two beautiful well behaved children, a nice little home in a beach city; My husband made a good living; I didn't have to work; I was a homemaker. Now my happiness was contingent on raising a family...

Theme:
Happiness is based on being a successful wife and mother - A Real Woman!

Well, wifedom and motherhood had its rewards, and yet they were not totally fulfilling me, so I decided to get involved in community activities. I thought it was possible that happiness was dependent on being useful. I had read something - I think it was a magazine article - about purpose brought you happiness. I became active in progressive political movements and non-profit organizations. I organized successful fundraisers to support a day-care in a barrio, a candidate for president, farm workers in Delano, and scholarships to college.

Theme:
Happiness is based on being of service to your community.

That didn't work either. So what did I do? It was the 70's and the meaningful action was on college campuses. Yep! I went back to school. Maybe I'd be happy if I was intellectually stimulated, and associating with a diverse population, and involved in exciting new ideas. I majored in literature and history. I loved them both! I thrived in my studies. I met people from other countries and from all walks of life. I helped some of my fellow students by creating study circles.

Theme:
Happiness is based on gathering knowledge and being intellectually stimulated.

Nope! That did not give me the durable happiness I wanted.

I look back at all the many things I did to find myself and to become a happy person - and realize that they were all good things that gave me moments of satisfaction and happy feelings...they just didn't make me an intrinsically happy person.

I didn't know what else to do. People enjoyed my company. My husband and I entertained or went out with friends every weekend. I accompanied my husband to all his business social events and get-togethers. I went to all my kids' sports activities and did volunteer work. I had shown that I was intelligent...after all I got A's and B's in college. I drove a very nice car. I went to the best restaurants. I flew to Hawaii or Puerto Vallarta (the in destination in the 60's and 70's) for long weekends. I bought whatever I wanted when I wanted. And I was not happy...although everyone thought I was...because I had everything a woman could want! And since I thought I had everything a woman could want, I acted happy. After all, I knew how to smile. To let people, even my close friends know that I was unhappy, I believed, would make me look like an ungrateful bitch.

Then I had an imperceptible perception that had probably been brewing (no pun intended) for an extraordinarily long time...The effects of alcohol made me feel happy. And if drinking didn't make me happy; it made me care less if I was happy or not - so I drank more. Then I drank more, more often. Eventually, those habitual "happy times" and "carefree times" morphed into habitual "misery times."

I had done everything I had learned that was supposed to create happiness - why wasn't I happy? Why was I growing more miserable? Why did I think life was supposed to be something else? Something better? Maybe fulfilling? Even enjoyable? Something deep inside of me kept me searching for that something better. But I didn't know how or where to find it and I came to a point of desperation. I attempted to bring attention to my misery by making suicide attempts - all of which I botched - I didn't want to die. I wanted to escape the hell I was in and to feel free - free of pain, loneliness and unhappiness.

Included in my drinking habit was driving drunk, which I had done way too many times. I finally got stopped and jailed two times within a three month period. I believe that this was another attempt to reach out for help. I was starting to think I had a problem. My husband, family and friends didn't think I had any that was too serious or unusual. Yep. This kind of problem was "normal" behavior in our social circles.

The outcome in the first case was a plea bargain to reckless driving with a fine. However, the judge presiding over the second incident sentenced me to serve 15 months in a drivers' diversion program. This included: doing volunteer service for six months; maintaining journals of conversations about recovery and about all other areas of my life including: physical, intellectual, social, spiritual and emotional aspects; and a minimum of three meetings a week in a Recovery Program for 15 months. It was at those meetings that I found support and my first guides and helpers. I quit drinking. But initially I thought that I would resume it upon completion of my "sentence." Slowly, however, my thinking began to clear. I learned to identify my feelings, and I continued to move forward-tiny step after tiny step without a drink...one minute, one hour...one day at a time.

Eventually, I was able to begin to accept me and the prospect of "not drinking." I was given tools to discover my real self. And I began to use them. I completed a moral inventory of my shortcomings and resentments and my positive attributes as well. I learned to open up and trust through sharing that inventory. I made amends to those that I had harmed. I learned to pray and meditate. And I learned to be of service with an open and giving heart. From applying myself and working with all the tools provided me I received many valuable gifts. Two of the gifts were a belief in a Higher Power and the ability to laugh at my follies and character defects. With the help of those two gifts I learned that when I accepted myself I could take the next step and change the things about myself that I wanted to change - and that as I grew, my ability to look at myself would become easier. I even began to look forward to more of my shortcomings being revealed because I knew that I would have developed the necessary tools to deal with them. I felt gratitude for the Program, its tools and my willingness to use them. I felt love for my Higher Power, the Program, the fellowship that I had found, for my family, friends and myself, my outlook was more positive and I was enjoying giving and receiving compliments.

And so it has been. I have grown even more self-accepting and self-loving. As I have become increasingly aware of my internal world and how it operated . . . my thoughts, feelings and spirit...I have come to understand that happiness has been evolving within me. After 30-plus years of well-guided and misguided self-evolvement, I have felt it growing deeper inside of me . . . intrinsic happiness. I sometimes have had the sensation throughout my being that I was satiated with bliss.

I now sometimes feel as if I am going to burst with joy and I often find myself saying out loud, "I am so happy." My happiness often oozes from me , heartening friends, family and other people who pop in and out of my presence. This is finally it... a sustaining happiness living in my core.

When I look back it is clear to me that I had to search for happiness in all the places outside of me to discover the limited, insufficient value of extrinsic happiness before I could move along on my journey to my intrinsic happiness. I now have come to embrace it as part of my essence.

> *Happiness cannot be traveled to, owned, earned, worn or consumed. Happiness is the spiritual experience of living every minute with love, grace, and gratitude.*
>
> — Denis Waitley

Suggested Exercise

I invite you to write a list of beliefs you may have about what creates happiness.

Choose one belief from your list that you want to change and explore the ways that you can transform it into a viable belief for you today.

Extrinsic and Intrinsic Happiness...

> *Genuine happiness can only be achieved when we transform our way of life from the unthinking pursuit of pleasure to one committed to enriching our inner lives, when we focus on 'being more' rather than simply having more.*
>
> — Daisaku Ikeda

Extrinsic Pleasure Happiness compared to Intrinsic Authentic Happiness is like consuming yummy, carb-loaded foods and beverages full of sweet tasting sugar compared to consuming healthier foods and beverages full of substantial tasty nutrients. Sugar-based foods give immediate pleasure but not a positive diet for meeting your body's needs; they also can leave you compulsively wanting more of them. Nutrient-based food is a positive diet that fulfills your body's needs, leaving you with a deliciously satisfied experience. Pleasure Happiness is served up with good feelings that last for only a few short moments, often leaving you craving more. Intrinsic Happiness is gradually but steadily absorbed into your very being, and leaves you feeling healthy and deeply satisfied with life in general.

To be clear, I like pleasurable moments and foods very much! A windfall of extra cash gladdens my pockets; a lovely chocolate soufflé delights my senses. But I now know such pleasures are transient and not meant to be given high priority in my life.

There is the belief that if something makes you happy; more of it will make you happier. For me it used to be - if one drink would make me feel happy, 10 would make me feel happier, longer! Wrong, of course! Have you ever felt that if having money made you happy then more would bring you even more happiness? Or... if some attention made you feel good, more attention would make you feel even better? That if being around someone made you feel happy, then being with them all the time would make you happy all the time? I do not know about you or anyone else...I do know that none of this worked for me! Happiness doesn't grow with more of the same extrinsic gifts from people, places or things that bring delightful but fleeting pleasure and momentary feelings of well-being!

Pleasure Happiness and Authentic Happiness, based on my experience, have different purposes. Pleasure Happiness serves me extrinsically and moves through my life. Authentic Happiness is an intrinsic part of my essence; it is planted and grows within me. The important thing is to be aware of the difference.

Suggested Exercise

If you wish, this is a good time to make two lists-one containing what creates your *Intrinsic Happiness* and the other containing what creates your *Extrinsic Happiness.*

Creating an Image of Happiness...

> *The only thing that will make you happy is being happy with who you are, and not who people think you are.*
>
> — Goldie Hawn

I got caught up in creating the "right image" - of a fun-loving, happy mother and wife that was intelligent and active in the community... successful and content with my life.

As I once did, I now have a few friends and acquaintances that have created "images" of themselves as having financially successful lives that make them happy. A couple of them have actually shared with me that they are not as happy as they think they could be and do not understand why they are not more content since they have more than enough money to live very well for their entire lives. I empathize with them and share my experience. I hope it helps.

Here is another image I once put on and continue to come across... have you ever come across those who create an image of a "happy" family who enjoys doing everything together? Now that's not to say that some families do not enjoy doing things together; of course families can have a great time together. I am suggesting that there are folks who form an image of having a happy family by putting out the message, (we love doing things together), crafting an image that is not based on reality. It is an effort to mask unhappiness or discontent by presenting a false image. I know - I did it for a long time.

These image masquerades are generally not created consciously... I certainly didn't realize what I was doing. They are merely attempts to be what we think we are supposed to be in order to be in good standing in our community...to belong - to be accepted.

There are countless images we create to show the world that "We are okay folks - successful, happy." The thing is, an image is just an image, and false images can be a really formidable barrier to true happiness.

I learned that when the outside image created is based on the reality of the situation and a reflection of an internal experience then it is honest and authentic - happiness can grow there - the outsides match the insides; and when it is created to obscure the internal truth then it is simply false - and authentic happiness cannot grow in an ingenuous milieu where the outsides don't match the insides.

Sharing...A Reciprocal Flow

All who joy would win must share it. Happiness was born a Twin.

— Lord Byron

My happiness seems to grow in direct relationship to the amount of happiness I share with others.

Sharing happiness has become effortless and natural as it flows from me, permeating the atmosphere around me for others to enjoy.

That happy energy I share flows back to me from those who receive it. It is a joyful exchange, although it is not the intent or expectation.

Today share a happy thought with someone!

Today as you are walking, driving or sitting in a group, think about a happy thought that you can send visualize it flowing out into the environment around you!

Take in kind words, smiles, gestures and beauty and absorb them into your being!

Suggested Exercise

You are invited to explore the images, if any, that you created to project being happier than you really are.

List the false images you have crated and then write an authentic way of being for every false image you have found yourself caught up in.

I accept my life.
I am grateful for my life.
I love my life.
I attend to my life.
My spirit soars.
And so can yours!

Suggested Exercise

Happiness is diverse. It is different to different people. What does happiness look like coming from you? You can write a description or a poem; draw a picture or make a collage from cut-outs. Remember it is about "coming through you," not "coming to you."

Four Virtues, Spirit and Happiness

Growth itself contains the germ of happiness.

— Pearl S. Buck

I was unaware that four virtues-Acceptance, Gratitude, Constructive Attention and Love-were the nutrients of my authentic happiness until about three years ago. What I did know was that I was the happiest that I had ever felt during my 70 years on this planet. (Goes to show you that it can just keep getting better.) I felt intrinsically happy. So it was clear to me that something had shifted inside of me and that something had triggered that shift. I began reviewing my life's journey-in particular the segment from the time I got sober at thirty-three until the present time. I found that I had been practicing these four virtues to varying degrees over the years. And I made a conscious decision at that moment to keep them growing in my life and to share what I had discovered. Then two years ago while I was driving around the country, I had an epiphany...I expressed these respective virtues in a range of tones - sometimes passionately, sometimes seriously, sometimes gently, and so on. During a reflective moment as I was parked on the side of a country back road, looking at the beauty around me, I heard a quiet voice come from within me, "Your Spirit...everything you express is carried out into the world by your Spirit. You know-your Energy." Duh, I had known for years that it is energy that produces our attitudinal vibes.

As I continued to do my inner work, it became obvious to me, that the virtues of Acceptance, Gratitude, Constructive Attention, and Love boost each other's growth and fuel my Spirit by creating a dynamic looping of positivity that is a primary contributor to the shaping of my personality. My spirit... my energy force...transmits my expressions, which present my character and its attitudes to the world, in effect saying, "This is who I am at this moment." And who I am is charged with positive energy - thus my expressions attract more of the same positive energy (since "Like attracts Like" is a universal law). So it is that my Spirit, my energy force in its giving is also receiving positive energy - and so my Spirit becomes another source of positive nurturing energy for the four virtues and, therefore, my authentic happiness.

This dynamic flow creates a perennial garden of happiness with a reciprocal transmission between the four virtues and their agent, Spirit. And like any garden one plant may grow stronger under certain conditions than others. During those times that plant will become the primary producer. However, the others will still be tended to and reinvigorated until they reach their full potential. When I recognized this pattern, I understood that any one of the virtues can lead to the development of the others so you do not need to practice all of them at the beginning. You can start by focusing on the growth of one or two of the virtues of your choice and then the others will be germinated.

How consistently and energetically do you experience each of the Virtues working in your life? For instance, if I am grateful eighty percent of the time, I'd give Gratitude a ten. If I was grateful fifty percent of the time, I'd give it a five.

Suggested Exercise

On a 1-10 scale, how do you rate the strength of each of these attributes of happiness in your life today:

Acceptance -

Gratitude -

Constructive Attention -

Love -

If you do not give any one of them a 10...what do you need to do to make one of them a ten in your life?

An example using Gratitude again:

1) I will commit to writing a daily Gratitude Journal.

2) I will work at becoming more aware of what I am grateful for and acknowledge those things.

If you want to start consciously growing one or two of these Virtues, which will you choose?
How will you grow it?

A place for happy thoughts...

Chapter Three

. . . .

THE VIRTUE OF ACCEPTANCE

Acceptance doesn't mean resignation;
it means understanding that something is
what it is and that there's got to be a way
through it.

— Michael J. Fox

Acceptance as used here is about acknowledging the capacities, functions, and conduct of our inner and outer realms. Simply put, acceptance admits, "It is what it is!" Acceptance is not necessarily embracing something; it is acknowledging the existence of something – a situation, event, behavior or attitude related to self or others. It is recognizing a person, place or circumstance as being whatever it is. I realize that once I experience acknowledgment and accept someone or something, I am in a position to evaluate what I can change and what I cannot change. If I can change a thing then I take the steps necessary. If I cannot change it, then I can avoid it, or relate to it just as it is.

I soon realized that there was usually someone or something that I wanted to be different, in one aspect or another, but knew I did not have the power to make this change happen. So I learned to search out and focus on something positive about that person, thing or situation; then I was looking at something I did not want to change. It was a simple thing to do…it just wasn't easy! It did take my conscious commitment to make my life better by learning and practicing this application of conscious choice.

Acceptance is about jumping out of the world of the "right and wrong" and into the world of "different." I realized that when I was living from a view of "right and wrong"….right equated to acceptable and wrong equated to unacceptable. When I moved into a perspective of "different" then it wasn't about being "right" or "wrong" but just "is," and this taught me to be humble instead of being the "The Judge."

When I was growing up in my family being "right" was a basic value. If you weren't "right" then you were "wrong" and that was shameful. I used to study late at night so that I would have all the "right" answers when I went to school the next day because I believed that school was where you went to show what you knew; not where you went to learn. Mistakes were "wrong" and not tolerated in my home so mistakes were not admitted. We learned to hang on to being "right" no matter what…at the least you did not admit to being "wrong." It was a matter of not being shamed.

I remember an incident when I was talking with my father about something I had learned in history. What it was exactly doesn't really matter - that day, in whatever way that I shared with him what I had learned, he took a contrary position, explaining that I must have misunderstood or they were teaching me wrong at school. To prove my case I pulled out the encyclopedia and looked up the event we had been warring about and there it was in print exactly as I had told him. I handed the encyclopedia to him and showed him that it backed up what I was saying. My father looked at it, shook his head, smiled… and calmly said, "See that goes to show you even the experts can be wrong!"

Years later, as I was determined to change some of my unhealthy patterns, I practiced admitting I was "wrong" every time I found myself in a disagreement. I admitted being "wrong" even when I believed I was surely "right." I did this until it became easy to for me to concede that I was in the "wrong."

I gradually learned 3 major lessons:

1) There are few if any positions worth arguing about as being in the right or wrong.

2) Being "right" or "wrong" on a position does not make me "right" or "wrong" as a person.

3) Being "right" is not a basis for being proud and being "wrong" is not a basis for being ashamed.

Ultimately, I came to a place in my life where "right" and "wrong" merely meant having "different" views and actually had nothing to do with making me or anyone else "wrong" or "right." Accepting different views and ways of doing things relieves me of having to defend myself by trying to prove that my view or way is the right one. This is a load off my shoulders! I feel freer to be me.

Acceptance has an element of surrender...which leads to peace and, paradoxically, victory!

I often use World War II as an example of how surrender leads to victory. During the turning point of the war when the Allies began to take back fallen countries from Germany, the Germans continued to be in denial and gathered boys to fight; they executed thousands upon thousands of Jews; the Nazis continued to yell out slogans of victory for Hitler and the Motherland, and more and more cities in Germany were bombed to smithereens. Then Berlin was blitzed–flattened. Finally, the Germans were blasted out of denial and surrendered. Meanwhile, Japan was standing firm against the bombings demolishing their country, refusing to surrender. They continued to fight in the jungles and to fly suicide bombing missions fighting harder than ever against their inevitable defeat. Officers who could not accept the shame of defeat in battle committed hara-kiri. Then in August 6, 1945 Colonel Paul Tibbets flew the bomber Enola Gay over Hiroshima and dropped a 9,000lb A-Bomb. Still the Japanese did not surrender. So three days later on August 9, another bomber, called Bockscar, flown by Major Charles Sweeney, dropped a 10,000lb A-Bomb over Nagasaki on August 15, 1945 and Emperor Hirohito announced his country's surrender in a radio broadcast. The paradox is that both of these countries, once they accepted defeat and surrendered, received assistance from their victors…cleared away the wreckage across their lands…and rebuilt, becoming two of most successful superpowers in the world. A story of Acceptance-Surrender-Victory!

On a more personal stage, when I was in the very early phases of recovering from alcoholism I struggled with believing in a higher power. I struggled and struggled until one day a strange sensation came through my body. I felt like my intestines were being squeezed and pulled and I couldn't attribute it to anything. I didn't feel sick in any familiar way. I was scared. It grew more and more physically painful. I felt like running. I knew there was not anything medically wrong with me. My recovery program stepped in and I thought, "Call Dorothea" (my sponsor). I called her. She was not home. I called all my close friends on the program - no one answered their phone. I thought I was going to die - something so unfamiliar was happening within me - I was powerless. I was getting more and more scared. I called my mother. She didn't answer. I did not want to take a drink - Yes I did - but I didn't! I wanted to be free of the pain. My guts felt like they were tangling or untangling or both! I had no idea what was going on. I was alone, scared and in horrible pain. I took a deep breath. Then I went to my bedroom, laid myself on my bed and crumbled into a fetal position, whimpering - then quiet. I was sure that in some way I was dying. And from somewhere deep down inside of me I heard my pure unadulterated plea, "Help" fill the room. Less than a second later as I lay surrendered to my condition, I saw a warm soft bright white light in the corner of my bedroom ceiling moving towards me - slowly stretching into the shape of a hand reaching to me and then wrapping around me. All my pain was gone. I was in a blissful state of peace. Then the light vanished. I lay there in total calm - a state of peaceful surrender. And I moved from denial to acceptance of a Higher Power. What it is or how it works I don't know. I just accept that there is Grace.

I do believe the major antonyms for acceptance are denial, criticism, judgment and rejection.

Learning to Accept Me

> *Confront the dark parts of yourself, and work to banish them with illumination and forgiveness. Your willingness to wrestle with your demons will cause your angels to sing. Use the pain as fuel, as a reminder of your strength.*
>
> — August Wilson

During my young adult years, I was afraid to face the truth about who I was. I avoided me at all costs. A reliable way I could escape accepting "me" was to focus on others. So I developed a demeanor which allowed me to scan for what I deemed as okay and not okay about others.

I could easily slip into "the Fixer" role and tell others what was "right" and "wrong" about them and what they needed to change - even now I have to be vigilant about this inclination. I can still slip into it like a foot into a cozy worn-in loafer.

Back then I refused to look at anything in my life that threatened the picture I had created about my life being "perfect." I couldn't accept it being anything less!

Oh, the irony! The "Judge-and-Fixer" supported by my habitual drinking built walls between my outer self and inner self; between my authentic and deceitful self; between my thoughts and feeling and my actions. Thank goodness! This corrosive carving up of these various "me's" caused a crescendo of pain that ultimately motivated me to do something - anything - to escape it. I reached out for help! As a consequence, my long and arduous journey to acceptance, and eventually wholeness began...

When did I accept that I couldn't change someone else but that I could change myself? When did I get the idea of self-acceptance? I don't know exactly. I know it had to do with getting sober. I have a foggy memory of struggling to identify myself as someone with alcoholism. After endless meetings and repetitious introductions to others like me, I reluctantly accepted the idea that I suffered from the disease of alcoholism. Once I accepted that notion a door opened up to a life-long process, an uneven flow of change and growth in my conscious awareness - and in consequence my willing acceptance of my true, always evolving self.

Acceptance grew into a strong thread woven into the fabric of me. However, now and again, my ego frays that fabric! Then I can be enticed into a period of denial that I have to face, move through, and again surrender to my human imperfections to make way for my return to a conscious state of acceptance. This seems to be a regular part of my growth cycle.

The Principles of the Recovery Program taught me about acceptance:

1) To replace struggle with Acceptance that leads to surrender, thus replacing pain with peace.

2) That Acceptance is recognition that anything about me, about someone or something else is what it is, or how it is - Period!

3) That steady, conscious repetition can change habits.

4) Too many other valuable things to list.

Generalizing the concept of acceptance was no easy matter. The Serenity Prayer became my mantra. I repeated it throughout my days for a year and after that, as often as needed. I came to understand its meaning not only in my head, but at a heartfelt level - within my core.

> *God grant me the Serenity to Accept the things I cannot Change; the Courage to Change the things I can and the Wisdom to know the difference.*
>
> — Reinhold Niebuhr

I revisited the Serenity Prayer an infinite number of times and relearned acceptance in one challenging circumstance after another. Yes, I stumbled and bumbled between accepting and not accepting whoever and whatever I did not like or agree with or simply did not understand.

It is amazing how many different aspects of life there are where acceptance, or the lack of it, influences our outlook regarding our everyday living.

Suggested Exercise

It may be interesting to explore what your challenges to acceptance are. This could be a place to do that. Just write down the main things that are hard for you to accept and then write how each affects your life.

Hard to accept:

1.

2.

3.

4.

How this has affected my life:

1.

2.

3.

4.

If you decided to complete the previous exercise, then it may be a good idea to look at how your life would be affected if you accepted, and surrendered to, one of the challenges you wrote about.

Reread the Serenity Prayer, then explore what it means to you. Be as still as you can and absorb it. Take care to note what you believe Accept, Courage, and Wisdom mean in this context. List what you think you can change and what you think you cannot change.

If the need to be right and / or the fear of being wrong plays a part in your struggles to accept, you could explore that here:

Not Getting What I Want When I Want It or...
Looking Outside of Me for Happiness!

Remember that sometimes not getting what you want is a wonderful stroke of luck.

— Dalai Lama

There was a period - actually a pretty long period, like a decade or two - when I wanted a life partner more than anything. I prayed for one. I joined organizations to find someone. I enlisted myself into dating organizations that promised to find the right mate for me. Nothing happened. Then a special someone would come along and I would lose myself trying to make that one happy (so I could be happy). Although these relationships weren't good matches, of course I would stubbornly hang on to them, trying to make them work. And of course, like Cinderella's sisters, no matter how hard I tried, I couldn't make the shoe fit. I just created a string of unsuccessful relationships and unhappy moments.

One day, following yet another wrenching breakup, I decided to take myself to the beach. I love the ocean. It usually makes me feel better. I went to a quiet place I know of and sat on the sand and looked out at the endless sea. The horizon was its usual straight line. My eyes roamed over the vast bluish-green mass. I saw a bobbing fishing boat that looked like a bathtub toy. Then my ears followed the sounds coming ashore and my eyes explored the waves. A wave would rise up, roaring, roll into a tube that would then unfold its power and glide onto the shore.

Another...another... and another... one after another they continued to rise, rolling into a tube, unfolding and gliding, each making its own unique mark on the sand. Ah, I got it! I cannot make a relationship happen. I have to allow it to happen.

You see, once again I am shown that when I pay attention, the answer is there. Sometimes the answer may not be what I want it to be and sometimes it is better than what I expect. But whether I like it or not, I can count on it to get me out of confusion and into the clarity which nurtures my acceptance.

In this case, I learned that if we choose we can take an action and if we wait to see what unfolds from that action it will make its own unique mark on the shores of our lives! If we accept an outcome for what it is, we can then choose to embolden it or to allow it to fade away.

Accepting the Unacceptable: People, Places, Things and Me

> *You are imperfect, permanently and inevitably flawed. And you are beautiful.*
>
> —Amy Bloom

In my family of origin only three feelings were expressed: angry, happy, and caring. Loneliness, fear, sadness (except at funerals), and distress or disappointment (whining fell under disappointment) were not tolerated. So in the early stages of my sobriety and evolutionary journey, facing and learning to express the feelings that I was not familiar with was a definite challenge.

I remember the first time I clearly experienced the feeling of loneliness. I was in my living room, my two children were in the backyard with a friend, and suddenly, I felt this raw, vaporous emptiness flow through me - a discomfort and complete disconnection.

I was cognizant of the fact that my feelings were going to start to stir within me. Realizing that this could be a feeling coming through me, I decided to explore it. This is one of those times that I listened to my intuition…the wisdom within me. Though it was out of character for me, I lay down on the living room sofa, stretched out, and asked "What feeling are you?" And, I found myself responding "So you are loneliness. I want to get to know you." As I lay there, I scanned my body and expressed aloud what I was experiencing. "You feel like a balloon in my stomach; my throat is dry and wordless; my chest feels like it is empty, as if there is no heart in it, only the color yellow. This is very interesting. Thank you for letting me get to know you better." At that point, the lonely feeling dissipated and was replaced with peace…serenity. It was a glorious sequel to my acceptance.

Now sometimes someone or something gets on my nerves and I don't feel very good in my skin - that's when it serves me well to remember that ACCEPTANCE is simply recognizing what is. Other times it is me myself that gets on my nerves, and I feel terrible being me; I find me unacceptable. In my more enlightened times I can choose to make a decision to accept, or not accept, a significant part of me. Then I come to a place that most of us get to now and again, the Y in the road. This is where we decide to go to the right or the left, or to just stay put at the junction of the Y.

I remember how one particular Y in my life's journey provided me with some real angst. I had parked at the Y-junction for a long while and realized it was time to choose a path and get on with it even though either path would involve pain. Would I take the less desirable, less accepted/unapproved path that would wrap me in authenticity, but would bring me pain plus rejection? Or, would I take the conventional path that would wrap me in deceit and would still bring me pain, but also approval?

I had broken through some of my denial several years before and had come to understand that I was a lesbian. I had several relationships, none of which had lasted as long as my marriage to my husband. I still had not come out to my family. I had not fully accepted it...me! Another man had come into my life and wanted a relationship with me. Here was my opportunity to be in the mainstream again – or not.

At least I did know that I wanted to release myself from my quandary and get on with my life; it was time for me to commit to one path or the other. So I did what often worked for me when I needed to find an answer inside myself; I went for a walk in a park – Wildwood Park in Thousand Oaks, CA. I walked along a trail and onto a small wooden bridge that crossed over a creek. Somewhere in the middle of the bridge I stopped to look at a sycamore. This sycamore wasn't a regular sycamore; it was growing in a different direction than its fellow sycamore trees. It had changed its course and was growing out of the bank and had reached the other side, making a natural bridge across the creek.

I watched that tree for the longest time… and that tree and I had an insightful conversation that changed my perspective. A smile brightened my face. I had received the answer. I couldn't accept me because I had been judging me as bad, wrong, and unnatural. I had been attached to the possibility of negative results. And here this tree was, showing me that even though most trees grow vertically some grow differently, even horizontally. It let me know that trees that grow vertically can give shade, provide homes for birds and other critters, and possibly give fruit. Trees that grow horizontally can provide bridges; they can provide different food and shelter for different critters - and this contrast within the forest makes it more interesting, more beautiful. Being different was a part of our natural world; it was not bad, wrong or unnatural. Diversity is one of the most intriguing and vital parts of life. It fosters flexibility, growth and a more comprehensive, broad perspective.

My heart smiled. Peace, much like a caressing breeze, gently blew away the turmoil that had plagued me. I would walk the road of my truth. I could learn to love and accept me as I am - different than most and similar to many.

A Thought…

Acceptance diminishes conflict. Lack of conflict makes room for grace. Grace is the heart of peace. And, peace is a twin sister to love and gratitude.

I Get That…

> *Acceptance looks like a passive state, but in reality it brings something entirely new into this world. That peace, a subtle energy vibration, is consciousness.*
>
> — Eckhart Tolle

We cannot change other people, places, things; we can change our own behaviors, thoughts, feelings and perspectives.

Any aspect of our Self that we do not recognize and accept we cannot change.

Self-acceptance is a prerequisite for accepting everyone and everything else.

To genuinely accept others we are required to accept their imperfections! It's up to them to make or not make changes in their lives.

Acceptance is about letting go of judgment and our attachment to specific outcomes.

To accept life, it is essential for us to accept the uniqueness, diversity, and changes in all segments of existence.

Acceptance is necessary to love. It is the open door through which love is given and received.

Acceptance is an elemental quality of happiness. Whenever we accept something we are simply realizing that it is what it is!

The more accepting we become the more stress-free daily living becomes.

We will forever be practicing and evolving acceptance in our life, reducing our impulses to control other people, places or things.

Accepting I Can Be a Fool...

> *Try as hard as we may for perfection, the net result of our labors is an amazing variety of imperfectness. We are surprised at our own versatility in being able to fail in so many different ways.*
>
> — Samuel McChord Crothers

I have to tell you that starting back as long as I can remember I could not tolerate my imperfections or anything else that I didn't understand before acceptance became a part of my life. When someone pointed out a shortcoming or a mistake I made I would justify it, blame it on someone or something else, or use humor to diminish it. I defended myself well and continued for years to draw layers of protective curtains over the windows of my shortcomings - moodiness, dishonesty, egotism, ingenuousness, inferiority; I could increase this list ad infinitum.

When I accept one of my shortcomings I do not need to defend it. Hopefully, I can laugh at it and eventually choose to change or not change it. Developing this view of my character defects has greatly diminished the drama in my life. I hope the following examples are helpful to you.

As some of my friends are aware, I am multi-skilled. I can perform a variety of undertakings - none necessarily exceptionally well, but well enough. There are occasions when I get carried away with declaring, "I can do this" or " I can do that" until my enthusiasm has morphed into arrogance. I may see an eyebrow raise; a bit of eye rolling or yawning; hear a coughing cue that says, "Boring!" Or sometimes a good straightforward friend may just cut to the chase and say something direct like, "Carolyn, alright already, that is enough of what you can do," or sarcastically comment, "Okay, Carolyn, we know you can do everything!" No matter how I get the message, I twitch a little, then smile and say, "Ouch!" I squirm a little and then accept that I am sounding arrogant or self-important. Then I may say something like "Okay, I can get carried away and don't know when to quit. I apologize for being so self-absorbed!" Of course I have to make sure that things are clear so I add, "I can do those things, you know!" We laugh and no one is offended - I no longer need to defend myself from the truth or its delivery. I smile, knowing the message I'm receiving is coming from people who love me.

One of my worst habits that I work on all the time and improve only in small increments is interrupting people when we are in conversation. It is awkward since I have years of experience listening as a counselor - but somehow in the circumstance of social intercourse, particularly with close friends and family, I have learned to practice impatience and excitability to the point that I sometimes interrupt others instead of listening! To all my friends and family who have been so patient with this defect of mine, I express my deepest gratitude for your unconditional love and acceptance.

Bottom line, it is just a matter of being humanly imperfect and accepting it!

Accepting allows me to laugh (at least smile) at myself and laughing helps me to accept myself…to accept the boor in me…my own trickster, my own "Fool." We all have at least one and we might as well enjoy it because it's going to pop up now and then and throw us off balance - to keep us on our toes!

I accept the imperfections of leaves, trees, stones, and all the other gifts of nature. In fact, I see them as stunning!

Don't you think it is our imperfections that make us uniquely us? If I can accept me, it is far more likely I will be able to accept you.

To accept me means to accept all of me just as I am. When I accept a flaw in my Self, I can choose to change it or to let it be! I know this message may be redundant. It is just so important I think it demands repeating.

I call one of my Fools "Know-It-All." On the other hand, I also have a Wise One that I call "Knows Little-Always Learning." What do you call one of your Fools?

Suggested Exercise

You may wish to make a list of some of your Fools and their Wise One counterparts.

Fool:

Wise One:

Fool:

Wise One:

Fool:

Wise One:

Fool:

Wise One

I am what I am, so take me as I am!

— Goethe

Positive Affirmations

Today I accept all of me just as I am!

Today I accept others just as they are!

Today I accept life as it unfolds!

You may want to write some "Acceptance" affirmations just for you…

1.

2

3.

4.

Chapter Four

. . . .

THE VIRTUE OF GRATITUDE

We can only be said to be alive in those moments when our hearts are conscious of our treasures.

—Thornton Wilder

Gratitude, I believe, is one of the perennial seeds for the interwoven garden of happiness. It provides an enriched basis for happiness to begin, to develop and to be sustained. How does it do that? Well, if you're like me, and I'd bet we are not much different in this area, it triggers a "feel good" button when you receive a thoughtful deed or a desired item has been gifted to you. The key to heartfelt gratitude is readily receiving and remembering. When our hearts are open to receive and our minds retain the memory of the deed and good feeling, it helps us to sustain our attention on our positive experiences. This creates a cycle of: receive, take in and feel good experiences that nurtures gratitude and opens us grow more gratitude. This process sharpens our sights toward the many blessings that enrich our lives - and round and round it goes, creating a cycle of gratitude building.

When we embrace the gifts we receive and express the gratitude that we have built up within us we are also creating our own cache of positive offerings to pass on to others.

Being Grateful

To speak gratitude is courteous and pleasant,
to enact gratitude is generous and noble,
but to live gratitude is to touch Heaven.

— Johannes A. Gaertner

I figured out that it is not having gratitude but being grateful that helps create true happiness. Having is an objective value whereas being is a subjective value. Being grateful means it is a trait or a characteristic - it is part of me so when I give my gratitude I give a piece of myself. On the other hand, when I have gratitude for something or other I am usually giving thanks or experiencing gratitude in an external context of pleasantries - politeness. Clearly, there is nothing wrong with having gratitude and expressing it to someone, demonstrating good manners; it is just that this invites a pleasing moment for myself and someone else rather than kindling an internal condition of genuine happiness. BEING a grateful person is part of being happy in my soul, in my core self.

I want to absorb gratitude into my being so it becomes an integral part of me - a fundamental feeling that is supported by my thoughts and actions. I don't want to merely express courtesies - I want to experience the kind of gratitude that comes from deep in my heart. I know I AM IN gratitude when gratitude IS IN ME!

Suggested Exercise

You are invited to explore the following:

Are you Grateful for the GIFT OF LIFE itself?...for being alive here on earth?

Are you grateful for ALL THAT YOU ARE?
How do you express your gratitude for "being?"

For being YOU?

An On-Target Message!

We often take for granted the very things that most deserve our gratitude.

— Cynthia Ozick

This was a memorable event. I was with my daughter and son, ages 13 and 12 respectively. This was a very long time ago since both of them are now older than I was when I became a grandmother to their children. We were taking a friend, who had never been to a professional baseball game, to Chavez Ravine for a Dodger-Giant game. We were hungry and stopped at a popular Mexican food stand and got burritos to go. I was eating as I was driving and - Lo! It happened! Red chili plopped down creating a Rorschach blot all over my white Levi pant leg! Although we were running late, I egotistically insisted that we stop so I could clean my pants. I did. Then I made a fuss during the entire drive; I complained and carried on as if I would not be admitted to the game with soiled pants. My kids were upset and my friend unsuccessfully tried to calm me and restore a fragment of peace.

It was a beautiful sunny day and I didn't care. I was a dark cloud taking the shine out of my dear ones' anticipated fun time. When we got seated I was still a sour-puss. Not only my pants, but also my day had been soiled and everything was irritating to me. The game started and that's where my three companions tried to put their attention, attempting to ignore my intense negative attitude. I continued to act asinine about the glaring wet spot, trying to cover it up with my purse. After a time, I decided nobody was looking at me and so I put my purse down…and at that exact moment Jonathan Livingston Seagull flew over and dropped one that smeared green grunge across my entire white lap! My kids broke into uncontrollable laughter and my friend tittered. I looked at that shiny white seagull and at the three of them and - suddenly I let loose, joining them in the laughter, looking skyward, shaking my hand, spouting something like "Okay, God, I get the message! Thank you!" Then we all relaxed; I used a napkin to wipe off the seagull's muck the best I could. We enjoyed the rest of the game!

I had acted self-centered - complaining - thankless. It took what it took to stop complaining, but thankfully, at last I woke up to being grateful to have pants to wear; grateful for having two great kids and a patient friend that loved me even when I was an ass; grateful for being able to buy food; grateful that I had a nice car to drive us there; grateful that I could afford tickets for great seats to a Dodger game; grateful for the beautiful sunshiny day and especially grateful to a humorous Creator that sent a special delivery message to me because obviously I don't notice the more subtle ones! I guess this is what they mean by "Don't sweat the small stuff!" I'd like to tag on to this - "and be sure to celebrate all the great stuff."

From Complaining to Gratefulness

Gratitude is riches. Complaint is poverty.

— Doris Day

Before getting sober and getting a positive outlook on life, complaining was embedded in some of my friends' and my gossipy casual conversations. Here are some examples of the common recurring grumbling my friends and I gushed out into our world:

It's too cold! (69 degrees) It's too hot! (80 degrees).

He…or she…or they… are always late.

Where are you?.... You said you would be here at 5! (It's 5 minutes after)

My steak is too done!..... or…My steak is too rare!

I am so bored! Life is boring! There's nothing to do. I don't want to do that! Can't you think of something fun?

Damn traffic! I hate it! Where are all these damn cars going!

She's never home to take care of the kids.
Her nose is always in a book.

I clean and pick-up after everyone and they don't give a damn.

Work, work, work…all you do is work…there is never any time for us.

I hate my job. My boss is a jerk.

It's not fair! We don't do anything fun together !

Life sucks!!

Complaining was a sure-fire barrier to evolving into a grateful being! After a bit of struggle, I accepted that and transformed from a Complainer to an Appreciator!

Here's how I changed the aforementioned complaints into statements that support an attitude of gratitude:

It's 69 degrees…thank goodness I am not in Maine where it is below freezing!

It is hot today…I am so happy I have air conditioning!

They are always late…it gives me some extra time to relax before they get here.

Are you okay? I was expecting you at 5 and you are

always on the dot. I'm glad you are okay. Be safe and I'll see you when you get here.

Usually, I like my steak rare/done and today I like it just like it is...I am grateful to have someone else cook while I sit here enjoying myself.

It is really nice to have nothing that I have to do...I can just relax.

Thank you for your suggestions, I would like to know...how does that sound to you?

When there is traffic like this it's a great time to catch up with my book on tape.

She is so busy...I wonder if she needs help with the kids.

I am so grateful that she likes to read...I can count on her to recommend a good book.

I am grateful I have time to clean...I like a clean house.

I know how hard you've been working and to show my appreciation for all you provide, I planned a weekend get-away we both enjoy...

Although my job has become a major challenge, I am grateful to have it until I find something that I will enjoy more.

Since my boss is disorganized and is sometimes petty acting, I am happy that our paths do not cross very often.

I do not expect life to be fair…however, I can be fair in my dealings; it's good for me and for whomever I'm dealing with.

I am so grateful to have you in my life…it is fun just being with you.

I love my life!

What qualities are you grateful to have as part of yourself and your life?

Suggestions for Growing Gratitude

> *Gratitude helps you to grow and expand;*
> *gratitude brings joy and laughter into your life*
> *and into the lives of all those around you.*
>
> — Eileen Caddy

Once gratitude was part of me, I knew I had to grow it to keep it. Here are some of the things I did and you can do, to grow gratitude:

Start each day giving thanks!..."It is a brand new day…there has never been one like it before and there will not be one like it again. Today is unique. It is a gift of life to decorate as I choose!"

Be conscious of the Breath of Life! Think about breathing in, keeping the oxygen, and exhaling, releasing the carbon dioxide. How magnificent to breathe in the sustenance of life and to let go of a toxic gas! Sometimes it's fun to do this with a tree - consciously receiving oxygen from the tree and giving the tree the carbon dioxide it needs. It's a lovely, conscious way of sharing.

Be conscious of how we are connected to all other life on our Earth…in our Universe. Spend some time with nature 3-4 times weekly… You can do this in your neighborhood or yard… in your garden, getting to know a houseplant, a stone, or a flower a bit better. Write about what you see, smell and feel, about how you can relate to that plant, stone, flower or….

Express your love for life with an attitude of gratitude!

Every now and again think of every breath as sending a prayer of "Thank You" out to the Universe, to the Great Mystery…to God as you understand God.

> *Cultivate the habit of being grateful for every good thing that comes to you, and give thanks continuously. And because all things have contributed to your advancement, you should include all things in your gratitude.*
>
> — Ralph Waldo Emerson

Write a gratitude list every day for 30 days and continue to write one about once a week in a Gratitude Journal. Or in your Gratitude Journal write a short gratitude list of three to seven things and pick one to elaborate upon.

Write about how it affects you and what you like about it.

Here is an example of some of the things that I wrote in my Gratitude Journal:

I am grateful for my close relationship with the Great Spirit.

I am grateful for the relationship I have with my children.

I am grateful for good health.

I am grateful that my children and grandchildren are walking their journeys and learning how to love and be loved.

I am grateful for all my loving, supportive, and fun friends.

I am grateful for my positive attitude.

I am grateful for my sense of adventure.

I am grateful for my healthy mind and body.

I am grateful for all the beauty around me.

I am grateful to be conscious of the inter-connectedness of all that is.

I am grateful for my happy life in sobriety!

I am grateful that I have discovered the power of acceptance, gratitude, constructive attention, and love.

I am grateful for the real happiness that is deep down inside of me…

Thank you, Great Spirit!

Suggested Exercise

What might you put in a Gratitude Journal and which one will you choose to expand upon?

1.

2.

3.

4.

5.

6.

7.

Pick one and expand upon it. Describe how it makes you feel, how it improves your life, etc.

I Collect Quotes on Gratitude That I Read Aloud Regularly

I would maintain that thanks are the highest form of thought, and that gratitude is happiness doubled by wonder. — C.K. Chesterton

If the only prayer you said in your whole life was, 'thank you,' that would suffice. — Meister Eckhart

Gratitude is not only the greatest of virtues, but the parent of all the others. — Marcus Tullius Cicero

Gratitude makes sense of our past, brings peace for today, and creates a vision for tomorrow.
— Melody Beattie

Gratitude changes the pangs of memory into a tranquil joy. — Dietrich Bonhoeffer

Gratefulness is the key to a happy life that we hold
in our hands, because if we are not grateful,
then no matter how much we have we
will not be happy – because we will always want to have something else or something more.
— David Steindl-Rast

God gave you a gift of 86,400 seconds today.
Have you used one to say "thank you"?
— William A. Ward

Suggested Exercise

I invite you to use the following space to add gratitude quotes that resonate with you…

You may want to place one or more on your bathroom mirror where you can read it regularly. If you do this I suggest you keep them fresh – replace or add to them monthly.

Yes, I can!
I certainly can!
I can have
A gratitude-flower-heart
That shall remain open
At all hours.

— Sri Chinmoy

Chapter Five

. . . .

THE VIRTUE OF CONSTRUCTIVE ATTENTION

Tell me what you pay attention to and I will tell you who you are.

— José Ortega y Gasset

Constructive Attention is primarily about focusing on the positive aspects of people, places and situations and expressing that attention in a helpful, thoughtful and considerate way.

What I pay attention to plus the quality of the attention I give to it determines what grows and how it grows in my life. How I pay A-ttention telegraphs my IN-tention. If my intention is positive - compassionate, supportive, respectful, interested or curious and non-judgmental - then nourishing energy will flow from me. If my intention is negative - indifferent, critical, contrary, judgmental, confrontational, or generally insensitive - consuming energy will flow from me. So, you see, it is imperative that I aim to be consciously aware of "Where & How" I give my attention if I intend to encounter people, places and things in a constructive and healthy way and have happy relationships with them.

Where and how I place my attention I believe says more about me than it does about who or what I am giving my attention to. For example, where and how I pay attention lets me know whether I am acting uncompassionate or compassionate; self-centered or thoughtful; unethical or ethical; ungrateful or grateful; un-accepting or accepting; loving or hateful - and whether I am going to focus on problems or on solutions, on whether I am building good "vibes" or not in my part of my interactions with people, places or things. It is my compass for guiding my attitude as it goes from within me out into my external world. To achieve this attitude, I committed to being a constructive influence during my meet-ups along my life journey.

Not Paying Constructive Attention

When we are no longer able to change a situation - we are challenged to change ourselves.

— Viktor E. Frankl

Recently I presented a women's retreat in Abiquiu, New Mexico. I spent some time putting it together... finding the right location for a small group; gathering a small group of women that wanted to be there.

The retreats that I offer are intimate events where the participants usually have profound experiences and get to know one another very well, and often times they develop on-going supportive friendships.

For the first time in preparing for a retreat, I felt something in me was "off" around this one. I could not figure it out. I stopped trying and assumed (red flag - you know assuming makes and "ass" out of "u" and "me") things would fall into place...and they did fall...differently and in a place I had not experienced before.

I had rented a car for the gals to have transportation from Albuquerque Airport. They drove to Santa Fe where I met them at the Teahouse for lunch. When they arrived I felt a frenetic energy coming from them. I perceived each of them as having a very strong personality, along with their own agendas. I could not seem to get control of the situation so I stayed out of control, watching, trying to get a take on this small group of women. What I experienced was that they were basically demanding and didn't seem to care to operate as a tribe but rather wanted to fulfill their individual needs. All I could see is that they were not what I was expecting. One was sick off and on for two days; two wanted to go off and do their own thing; and one just wanted to find a way to tolerate the others; and the other two acted as if they were lost and trying to make the best of it all. I did a first on a retreat...I reacted! I didn't take my normal leadership role. I joined them by trying to control them at times and satisfy them at other times. I handed the reins over to them and did the opposite of what I teach and what I am now writing about: I judged each of them instead of accepting each of them; I was not being in gratitude and it showed; I was focused on character defects instead of strengths; I was not operating with love in my heart; my spirit was deflated and whiny. Oh, my! As one of the women later described it...It was the perfect storm.

After a day and a half of this behavior, I reviewed what was going on with me by talking with a friend willing to listen. That helped me to get some clarity and I began to refocus. The next day I made some attitude adjustments. I made a very conscious effort to change what and how I was viewing them - I realized that I wanted to get to know these women and learn what they wanted and needed.

I was channeled into more of a balanced and harmonious viewpoint by guiding them around the *American Indian Medicine Wheel. During this process I connected to my authentic self and the rhythm of Spirit. This created a significant turning point and so the purpose for being at the retreat evolved. My attention turned fully to the positive, to the love, kindness and open hearts that flowed through each of these women. I was grateful to be in their company; the happiness in my heart awakened and warmed my soul - and hopefully touched them in some way.

Today I think of them and smile.

Oh! By the way, following the retreat I continued to look at my behavior...processed it...acknowledged and accepted my behavior for what it was...I didn't like looking at it...but it was mine to own. I knew my next step would be to share my self-discovery

**The American Indian Medicine Wheel, also known as the Sacred Hoop, symbolizes the flow and connection of all life and is used for healing -- balancing and harmonizing.*

with these women who participated in the retreat. The idea un-nerved me...I tend to resist setting myself up to be judged! It took a couple of weeks to gather some of them together to meet with me and when we connected I shared my insights and they shared theirs. Warm laughter danced through our conversation. It was as if we had gathered for one more hug.

To Be or Not to Be Honest - That Is the Question

> *Every year of my life I grow more convinced that it is wisest and best to fix our attention on the beautiful and the good, and dwell as little as possible on the evil and the false.*
>
> — Richard Cecil

I became aware of the changing power of constructive attention when I was working on becoming a more honest person - Yep! There was a time when I wasn't! It was a simple - and challenging process. I focused on being honest and when I slipped up I acknowledged it to myself and sometimes to someone else and then I made my amends. (Which means I didn't just apologize; I explained what I needed to change to practice honesty and what I was doing to change.) After countless amends and corrections, while maintaining a focus on being honest, I actually grew into being a basically honorable person.

Following is an example...

One of the first things suggested to me by folks in my Recovery Program was to focus on being rigorously honest. They emphasized that honesty was absolutely necessary if I was going to stay sober. I think truthfulness is a must if you are going to make any successful change towards a more authentic life.

I remember an incident at our local Alpha Beta Supermarket during the days when there were such things as Alpha Betas. Like many times before, one day I went through the checkout stand at this local Alpha Beta and as I was exiting, I scanned my receipt - a habit I picked up after I once paid for something that wasn't in my bag when I got home. And this time I discovered that I had not been charged for a bunch of asparagus. For a moment, I thought, "Yeah! I win one!" Then I started thinking about my focus on honesty. Then the committees in my head began debating between fixing the error and rationalizing that at times I had probably overpaid and this was just natural justice at work. The question arose about whether or not I am going to live from truth: Am I going to practice honesty or not? The answer was yes, I am! I remember having a wonderful freeing feeling stirring inside me when at last I resolved to go back and make it right.

I approached the cashier at the checkout stand and explained the error. She gave me a surprised look, then smiled and thanked me for being so honest. I not only felt good, I felt genuine connections, to the cashier and to my own growing integrity.

Umpteen years later...I am shopping at Target in Santa Fe, New Mexico. I have a basket full of stuff and check it out. I get to my car and am unloading my bags of stuff when I spot a small package that's caught in the cart. I empty the cart, take it back to the cart collection area, take my package to the cashier, and tell her that the item wasn't paid for when I checked out because it was stuck in the cart. She responds, "Yes. Things like that happen." And just rings it up. There was no surprise in her voice or on her face; it was as if I had done what anyone would do.

Later on I realized that this was exactly as it should be. We both just focused on honesty as the natural state of affairs. Nothing special...I had merely reinforced the practice of acting on my values. Honesty grew stronger in my life because I was focused on behaving with natural honesty instead of struggling with dishonest behavior. I was also focused on feeling good about myself and my positive behaviors and I knew an honest act would always help me to feel good about me.

Remember, all this is about progress, not perfection. Now I estimate that I practice being honest most of the time. The other times remind me that I am not perfect and can keep working on it!

One of my mantras is "Where my attention goes, my energy flows; where my energy flows is what I am surely going to grow."

Paying Attention

I see the dry grass bunched in the beak of a flicker,
I hear the mice playing tag in the woodpile
I feel the cold sneaking in through the windowpane
I taste the turmeric sprinkled thru my jasmine rice
I smell the fresh dung dumped by a neighbor's horse
I know the sweet and barb of the prickly pear
I dance to the ebb and flow of the endless shores
You see...
I had stood on the portico and knocked on the door
Life clearly greeted me; and I greeted it right back.

You can choose to examine where and how you give your attention. You are invited to consciously focus on something that makes you feel good about you. See if you feel your heart grow lighter. Do you feel freer and less burdened? Whatever you feel, it will most likely be better! Now give your constructive attention to what you love about you! Express it! Sing it, draw it, write it, dance it!

Where Does Your Attention Go During Transitions?

How strange that the nature of life is change, yet the nature of human beings is to resist change. And how ironic that the difficult times we fear might ruin us are the very ones that can break us open and help us blossom into who we were meant to be.

— Elizabeth Lesser, *Broken Open: How Difficult Times Can Help Us Grow*

Every transition is both a losing and gaining process, whether it seems basically to be a welcome transition or a painful one. It is up to us to choose how much attention we give to the pain of loss and to the rewards of gain. I believe we have to give some attention to our loss; let ourselves feel the pain...then we must gradually turn our attention to what we gained, whether that be memories, lessons, financial security, freedom, wisdom, and so on. Remember we want to give our attention to what we want to grow in our lives. Chances are that if we are looking at our loss too often or too long we will get stuck in it and it will grow into resentment or depression; if we give our attention to what we gained it will grow into gratitude and love.

We have lots of losses during our lives. Some we may experience more deeply and consciously than some others. We lose people who move on from this earthly life; we lose people with whom we part ways; we lose jobs, opportunities, money and dreams; we lose parts of ourselves such as: beliefs, health, ideals, attitudes, behaviors and habits, perspectives, feelings, lifestyles, skills and communication styles; our figures...our taut skin, perky tits, six-packs and tight asses. Losses like these move through our lives so insidiously that we don't even realize they're happening. But some losses get right up into our faces... like losing a wallet with all our credit cards in it!

Often the things I have gained from my losses have been much more subtle than the losses themselves. Sometimes it has taken me weeks, months and even years before I recognize, understand and accept the rewards left by a particular loss. But then the benefits seem to unfurl like the leaves of the cottonwoods during springtime.

I remember my first significant loss. I was about six or seven years old and I was in the kitchen with my great-grandmother, Minta Mackey. I had gotten dressed for school and my grandma had braided my hair and was fixing Cream of Wheat for me like she did most mornings. Then suddenly she stopped stirring my oatmeal on the stove and dropped to the floor. My heart stopped and I went to her side and asked what was wrong. She quietly said, "Toody (my family nickname), go get your Aunt Suveda and then you go to school." I got my aunt and hurried her back to my house. I told my grandma that

I didn't want to go to school. I wanted stay with her. But she insisted and I didn't want to upset her so I went to school. At the end of my school day, I ran home to see how my grandma was. And, when I got on my block I was met by my neighborhood friends yelling at me, "Toody, they took your grandma away." My heart was beating so fast. I was scared. What would I do without my grandma? She had been my caretaker, my security. I ran home as fast as my legs could go.

I do not remember much after that except that I visited my grandma a few times in what was called a "rest home" during those times. Then she passed on in 1953. They let me say good-bye at the mortuary but I was not allowed to go to the funeral. I had lost my grandma the morning when she fell to the floor and I went off to school.

For years I focused on my great-grandmother's stroke being my fault because she was getting me ready for school and I resolved that it was just too much for her. If only I had gotten myself ready and let grandma rest...

The day came when I began to think of my grandma and did not focus on her in the kitchen fixing me oatmeal. Instead, I remembered her holding my hand as she walked me to Friends Church every Sunday. I remembered her sitting in the rocking chair weaving rags (that she asked us all to save) into beautiful rugs. My grandma was the first recycler I knew. I remembered that she cared for the chickens and the vegetable garden. I remembered how she baked, especially the smell of brown bread; and how she cooked everything from scratch. I remembered that my grandma always made extra and took it to someone who was ill or in need. I remembered how my grandma, whom I shared a room with, closed each night with a prayer followed by us singing three hymns - each night she would ask me to pick the hymns and each night I would pick two different hymns and the last hymn I chose would always be Silent Night. I remembered my grandma always saying, "Thank you, Toody." Not once did my grandma mention that I picked the same song, a Christmas carol, for the last song of the evening. I remembered that my grandma never complained and always said kind things about people. Today I cherish the gift of memories and teachings my grandma left me. That is what I give my attention to today. Those memories spark a smile.

Two major terminations in our lives are often experienced as failures... jobs and marriages. Here, I must interject that I do not believe in "failure," a word that apparently has the connotation of missing the mark rather than searching for it. I agree with Thomas A. Edison when he said, "I have not failed. I've just found 10,000 ways that won't work." Somehow we have come to believe that we are not only "supposed" to keep marriage and jobs forever, but they each are "supposed" to get better and better. Our marriage is expected to grow more secure and comforting and we are expected to advance up the ladder in our careers...both marriage and career seem to be recognized as realms that require loyalty, dependability, responsibility and ability. During my lifetime, reality has shown us that sometimes that's the way the story unfolds and sometimes it is not - the story can take some unexpected turns.

Like my marriage. It was a fairy tale that lost its way and ended up on the shelf of horror stories. We had a model 1960's - 70's middle class suburban lifestyle laced with a good deal of partying. Then I stopped drinking - he kept drinking. I got deeper into living sober, finding my Self and he got deeper into alcohol, drugs and losing himself. We simply came to a place in our marriage where we went in different directions and grew apart. We both gave up the marriage in favor of our chosen paths. My price was loss of funds and other assets including our home, which became his. I lost my parents for a while, some acquaintances permanently. My children stayed in their home. We both lost them - me, for a while; him, forever later on.

The only thing I missed was my children not living with me.

During this time I was focused on telling my friends (my parents and other family members were not speaking to me) all the bad things about John, my estranged and soon to be ex-husband. After all I was trying to get healthy and he was obviously a drunken, druggy scum-bag who hid all his assets in a business and his money in safe deposit boxes, and refused to give me a dime in child support if I tried to take the children or house away from him. After all, he explained, he wasn't the one who wanted a divorce - it was my decision to leave, and I could take my personal things and what I needed from the furnishings and that was all.

My lawyer at the time seemed to think that John was being fair. For a while I held a bit (a minimization) of anger toward both of them. I felt cheated. Then I came to a place where I realized I could keep hanging on to that anger for as long as I wanted. I am blessed with good hearing. I kept hearing my sober friends' message, "Anger doesn't hurt the person you are angry at. They just go on doing their life. You're the one carrying the anger - the pain - so it only hurts you and they are going on without even thinking about it." Then I got it...this matter of being the bitter ex-wife stuff has got to stop. It would serve me well to get over it. I wrote about it. I started saying, "It is what it is." Then I began writing about all the good things in my 17 years of marriage. At the top of my list were, and are, my children. I began focusing on "if there was no other reason at all to be in my marriage, it was to bring two wonderful people into this world." Paying attention to that thought diminished my anger but some anger held on, lingering in my depths.

I think it was in 1992 when John, my ex, was in a coma, dying from alcoholism, when the 360-degree turn took place - I walked right by his room because I didn't recognize him. I then felt a different kind of loss. I was experiencing the loss of the dreams we had shared and never realized. I saw him lying there only 51 years old and looking 81. He was bloated and his hair was stark white. I looked at him and thought, "There, but for the grace of God go I." The children were with me and I suggested that each of us take some alone time with him and each have our closure. I went in last. I told him what I would have liked him to have done differently and I thanked him for specific gifts that he gave me. I forgave him and forgave me - and I forgave us both for all the harm we did to ourselves, to each other and to our children. And I stepped out of that room feeling lighter. My anger was gone and I felt room for the love to grow in me.

Later, over many years, other positive reasons for that marriage came to light and as they showed themselves, I added them to my positive thoughts of having my children, and gratitude grew for all that I got from that relationship. If it had not been part of my story, the chapter I am living today may not have become as rich and rewarding as it is.
I am aware of the endless transitions life brings us,

and I get that life is a series of modifications - that changes are perpetual. I can see clearly how with every loss I was given a gift.

Suggested Exercise

Questions you may choose to ask yourself:

What losses do I give attention to? How does it affect my attitude?

What gifts have been left for me by people and things I have lost?

How am I giving attention to the things I want to grow?

Suggested Exercise (continued)

Write a letter to yourself about what you want more of in your life and how you plan to pay attention to it.

The Mindset of Attention

When we talk about understanding, surely it takes place only when the mind listens completely - the mind being your heart, your nerves, your ears - when you give your whole attention to it.

— Jiddu Krishnamurti

Taking steps to change a perspective... to change anything at all...could possibly be the greatest challenge for us humans. I wonder if this is the main reason for the high sales of self-help books today - folks looking for an easy way to do what's hard... change! It is as if we want to read the books and have the information magically transport us to the top of the mountain. I did try this, actually quite a lot, and was always left with disappointment that it didn't work!

We tend to gaze up at the evolved guru at the top of the mountain and applaud, yearning to be up there with him or her. But when we take a look at that climb to the top, too often we get discouraged and tell ourselves, "It's too much for me" - and we give up and retreat.

It may be a better idea that when we give up the climb, we turn our focus to where we are. Focusing on where we are NOW is a better move than wantonly gawking at where we've been and fixating on where we want to be. Chances are that when we stop and are still, we are more likely to conjure up a new impetus - and may possibly choose to continue the climb without attachment to or expectation of the outcome. Or we may decide that where we are right now at this given time and place is good enough, at least for a while. Remember, that we are in pursuit of progress, not perfection.

My attitude at the women's retreat in Abiquiu reminded me that I cannot become complacent, that when I think I have arrived at the top of the mountain all the old attitudes can rear their ugly heads - and do! After all, thinking "I have arrived" is rather grandiose and unrealistic since the mountain I am climbing has no zenith; it has an infinite number of high points. It is in my best interest to remember that I reach for improvement...positive change...not perfection.

I must stay alert and appreciate that I am continuingly forming and reforming my perspectives to strengthen new optimistic attitudes born out of positive thoughts that I express through my actions. It is totally my responsibility to not linger in complacency, to maintain due diligence. It is also totally my responsibility to remember that all I strive for can be shoved aside by some of my old, familiar negative thinking that promotes undesired cynical attitudes. When it happens that I slip into negative thinking it is up to me, nobody else, to return my attention to the positives and regain my direction toward my desired path.

I accept that I am imperfect and will not, as I have learned from my sobriety program, "maintain anything like perfect adherence" to my principle of commitment to the virtue of constructive attention. What I can do is to keep aware of my vulnerability and tendency to get off track - and when I do, I can simply recommit to pay attention to positive aspects of each thing that occurs because I want my positive thoughts and attitudes to grow, and in turn, to nurture and build esteem instead of spreading negativity that disparages and devalues. Over and over again I consciously choose to pay constructive attention to all that I value around me at a given moment..."in the now" so what I love proliferates in my life. Thus I can continue the process of evolving myself into an authentically happy being!

There is a simple, fundamental reason so many new thought gurus and people in my profession are giving so much attention to the idea of changing our thinking from negative to positive and making attitude adjustments. Plainly put, it's because what's going on inside of us eventually shows up outside. And too often what shows up causes us problems that are wounding to our spirit - our life-energy and to the well-being of those around us. This is not about being good or bad, right or wrong...this is about not paying attention at all or putting our attention on the stuff that doesn't work for us...not recognizing that we have choices about this - and that how we think makes a difference. Positive thinking leads to positive attitudes and actions. Negative thinking leads to negative attitudes and actions. That is just the way it is. Let's accept it and be grateful that we can change our thinking and can change where and how we give attention. If we make this alteration we can heal spirits instead of wounding them.

I recently received the following humorous story through social media:

A woman in a supermarket is following a Grandfather and his badly-behaved 3 year-old grandson. It's obvious to her that he has his hands full with the child screaming for candy in the candy aisle, cookies in the cookie aisle and for fruit, cereal and soda in the other aisles. Meanwhile, Grandpa is working his way around, saying in a controlled voice, "Easy, William, we won't be long . . . easy, boy." Another outburst and she hears the grandpa calmly say: "It's okay, William, just a couple more minutes and we'll be out of here. Hang in there, boy." At the checkout, the little terror is throwing items out of the cart and Grandpa says again in a controlled voice, "William, William, relax buddy, don't get upset. We'll be home in five minutes, stay cool, William." Very impressed, the woman goes outside where the grandfather is loading his groceries and the boy into the car. She says to the elderly man, "It's none of my business, but you were amazing in there. I don't know how you did it. That whole time you kept your composure, and no matter how loud and disruptive he got, you just calmly kept saying 'things would be okay.' William is very lucky to have you as his grandpa." "Thanks," said the grandpa, "but I'm William. This little shit's name is Kevin."

Grandpa accepted that he could not control his grandchild...so he focused on controlling himself... giving himself supportive, compassionate messages. The result was that he calmed his spirit and raised the spirit of the woman in the market - and did no harm to the boy!

Paying positive, non-judgmental attention - Constructive Attention - to our own Self in relationship to people, places and things allows us to enrich our Selves as we travel along our way - growing happier and, maybe, wiser. Moreover, our doing this fosters positive feelings and behavior in those with whom we interact, since we have avoided blaming or criticizing them for whatever is going on and have dealt only with our own desire for positive and growth-producing interactions. However, most of us have for a multitude of reasons developed the opposite position - Destructive Attention. Destructive Attention is stocked with negative judgment, intolerance, criticism, recurring blame and branding belittlement. We display it in habitual gossiping, whining, and complaining. And we too often secretly suffer from the endless harassing echoes of a mindset that is often referred to as "negative self-talk." Now that said, it is up to each of us which kind of attention we primarily practice. Remember, getting a realization plus making a choice can be life changing.

For instance, if we recognize the following ways we practice Destructive Attention and choose to alter any one or all of them we can diminish their presence in our life by simply practicing more Constructive Attention:

When our attention is delivered with negativity, whatever we focus on grows increasingly distressful in our life and we most likely create unhappy experiences for ourselves and others.

When we passively place our attention on something by thinking negatively about it - whether it is something about us, another, or a situation - we are goading it to become more ubiquitous in our life, growing our discontent.

When we give our attention with loathing or disregard, we are behaving harshly and nurturing despair, antagonism and dislike in our interactions, encouraging more nastiness and discord in our life - and in our world.

Or, if we instead recognize any of the following ways we do practice Constructive Attention and choose to expand any one or all of them in our life we can consciously practice them more often:

When our attention is delivered with positivity, whatever we focus on grows increasingly gratifying in our life and we most likely will create happy experiences for ourselves and others.

When we put our passive attention on something by thinking positively about it, it becomes more prevalent in our life, cultivating our happiness.

If we give our attention with love and compassion, nurturing well-being and sincere support in our interactions, we encourage more beauty, peace and happiness in our life - and in our world.

Inevitably, paying Constructive Attention leads to a deeper sense of connection with our own Self and all other life, supporting the growth of genuine happiness.

A bonus is that Constructive Attention coupled with Acceptance fosters a view that all is well with the here and now - and that in turn can ignite a consequential Gratitude that can inspire Love.

Suggested Exercise

You are invited to do two practices:

1) If a time comes when you realize that you are focused on a negative thought, stop and think about something that you experienced that felt wonderful.

2) Each evening before bedtime write 3-7 things that you did that day that were positive...they can be simple things like getting to work on time or saying a cheery "hello" to your neighbor. The point is to start recognizing the good stuff about yourself that you too often minimize or disregard...you can expand positive thinking about you! The more positive thoughts you have about yourself, the more positive thoughts you will have about others and everything around you.

Loving Attention

There is a magnificent, beautiful,
wonderful painting in front of you!
It is intricate, detailed, a painstaking labor of
devotion and love! The colors are like no other,
they swim and leap, they trickle and embellish!
And yet you choose to fixate your eyes on the
small fly which has landed on it! Why do you do
such a thing?

— C. Joy Bell

Years ago I was seeing a couple in conjoint therapy. Although they had complaints about each other, they were obviously deeply committed to one another. Some of their complaints indicated that they were each focusing on the behaviors that their partner practiced that drove them up the wall. On one occasion, the wife had to excuse herself for a minute from the session to tend to some business.

While she was out of the office, the husband started complaining about a particular habit of hers. He said something like, "I know it is silly. It shouldn't be a big deal. But every time I see her [doing this] it makes me crazy. Sometimes, I think that I may have to leave her over this, as ridiculous as it may sound. I can't stand it!" When he was finished laying out his complaint, he surrendered, "I don't know what to do about it. What should I do?"

I remember suggesting something as simple as "When she is doing that - don't look at her!"

Some 15 years later this charming gentleman came to visit me and told me that my simple answer had saved his marriage. I was intrigued that such a simple suggestion had delivered a life changing impact. He explained that he had stopped watching his wife do what he detested and got himself focused on something else, and that small adjustment had made all the difference and saved his marriage. He happily reported that he loved his wife more each day. He had learned that where his focus flows is what grows in his own life.

I happen to know that for years this gentleman has given Constructive Attention to his wife. He pays attention to her strengths: intelligence, style, kindness, business sense, compassion, commitment, social grace, dedication, humor, wisdom and loyalty. How do I know this? He told me...and I have witnessed him many times expressing it to others. And I have seen his love and admiration for his wife bloom year after year.

He opened my eyes to the power of simplicity. Keep it simple. Where I look and how I look at something can make a life-changing difference. I will always be grateful to him.

A Thought I Ponder

Your living is determined not so much by what life brings to you as by the attitude you bring to life; not so much by what happens to you as by the way your mind looks at what happens.

— Kahlil Gibran

Undesirable things in life that we pay attention to can be the stimulus that opens our eyes to the "desired" or "good" things to which we are not paying attention.

For example: The man who was paying significant attention to his wife's "harmless quirky habit" may not have discovered he could choose where he placed his attention if he had not been driven bonkers by giving attention to something that irritated him to the point of putting a wedge between him and his wife. Once he realized he had a choice and decided to give his attention elsewhere, the wedge was dissolved and they grew closer.

Suggested Exercise

You are invited to explore: Do you have an example of experiencing something similar? If you choose, write what you learned from focusing on something undesirable.

Here are examples of what I do that helps me strengthen my Constructive Attention. You're welcome to try them:

Every time I focus on a thought that triggers a negative reaction - I acknowledge it. I smile at it. Sometimes it gets a laugh. Then I think of a positive experience that filled me with joy. I focus on staying consciously aware of "to what" and "how" my attention is being paid; to discern whether I want to change it; and then consciously change the focus of my attention to the "what" and/or "how" that I want to grow in me.

Each day I pay attention to the natural and human-made beauty around me...I soak it in. I talk to the flowers, sky, trees, birds, etc.

Each day I pay attention to three to seven things that make me feel good about me. At the end of the day I review them. They can be tiny insignificant every day kind of things like flossing my teeth, picking up the mail, calling my mother.

Each day I pay attention to my relationship with the Great Spirit.

Each day I pay attention to the kind interactions I have with folks.

Each day I pay attention to the gratitude and love I feel within me.

Each day I pay attention to how my feet, calves, knees, thighs, butt, abdomen, back, chest, hands, arms, shoulders, neck/throat, face, and scalp/head feel. I give each of them a good wiggle and stretch.

Each day I make effort to pay attention to my waking thoughts, give them a smile, thank them for their initiative and imagination; and adjust them if needed.

It's Not Easy!

> *We who lived in concentration camps can remember the men who walked through the huts comforting others, giving away their last piece of bread. They may have been few in number, but they offer sufficient proof that everything can be taken from a man but one thing: the last of the human freedoms — to choose one's attitude in any given set of circumstances, to choose one's own way.*
>
> — Viktor E. Frankl, MD

I know that some have walked this earth and have suffered unspeakable acts and for them it can be harder to turn their attention from the thoughts of these hideous experiences to more positive thoughts - even dreams. Yet, many do so in order to avoid the risk of losing everything.

If we pay attention to ourselves and change what does not serve us well, we can change our perceptions. If you want to perceive a challenging situation as impossible to solve or too big to overcome, then all you have to do is think, "There are no solutions; there is nothing I can do... nothing anyone can do." If you want to perceive a challenging situation as possible to solve, then you can think ideas like: "There has to be a solution; I can figure out some way to deal with this; I will ask around and find what others have done; I will pray and listen for an answer; I know there is a solution for me and it will come."

There may be times when we are in a situation where there is nothing that can be solved except how we handle it. We can choose to accept and find a way to live within our situation or deny that choice and/or struggle with it. If we accept that the situation is as it is, we can take care of our Soul, our Self, in a way that keeps it safe and strong. We can think encouraging thoughts about future possibilities, and think about any positives we can find in our lives and be grateful for any happy or peaceful moments, for any of the good and kind people that pass our way, the love we have to give, the beauty we have seen and will see again, our dreams for tomorrow. Paying attention to our positive memories and our dreams for our future - deciding to think only encouraging thoughts will plant seeds of dignity and strength and envelop us in some hope, and self-love.

An example of this self-motivated and stimulated positive perception in dire conditions is Nelson Mendela, who led his country out of apartheid and became its first President after spending two plus decades imprisoned. During that imprisonment he spent his time centered on what he could do for his country and developed a hopeful perception of the way things could be and how to make them that way - which he did!

Another model is Viktor E. Frankl, MD, PhD., who survived three Nazi camps, Theresienstadt, Auschwitz, and Dachau from 1942-1945, where he observed his and fellow inmates' attitudes and wrote notes on of bits of pieces of foraged paper. After his release in 1945 Frankl founded the treatment approach, Logotherapy, and wrote the inspirational book, *Man's Search for Meaning*, in which he writes about how he survived the horrific conditions in the camp by maintaining his focus on positive, hopeful, loving thoughts. *Man's Search for Meaning* has been considered one of the 10 most influential books in America.

I recently heard about Brook Axtell, a 34 years old survivalist of domestic violence who chose to reach out for help and eventually became the Director of Communications and Engagement for Allies Against Slavery (CEAAS), a non-profit devoted to ending human trafficking and the founder of Survivor Healing and Empowerment (S.H.E.), a supportive healing community for survivors of abuse, rape and human trafficking.

Then there is Mahatma Gandhi, who like Mendela, spent years imprisoned and kept a peaceful heart and planned for the freedom and future of India. He focused on whatever he was doing with forgiveness for those who persecuted him. He focused on his love for India and all her people. And, he smiled a lot.

Now thinking about smiling takes me back to 1991 at the Lensic Theater (Today known as The Performing Arts Center) in Santa Fe, NM. I was attending a conference for Marriage and Family Therapists being held at the Eldorado Hotel down the street from the Lensic. It happens that the Dalai Lama was in town during that time and requested to address us and so we were asked to gather at the Lensic for that event. Like every other conference attendee I was excited beyond words. Why did he want to speak to us? Well, basically what he said to us is that he wanted to talk with us because as therapist we impact many, many people and he wanted us to know that we should not take life so seriously and should help our clients to laugh more and to have happy hearts. He explained that he had to leave his country and that he missed and cared very much for all his people who were left behind in Tibet, and yet, he knew everything would be okay. He explained that no matter what our pains, laughter and happiness healed the heart and mind. I will always remember the laughter and the sparkling eyes that came from this man who was driven from his country and could have been broken-hearted, but instead was filled with love and joy.

We can occupy our minds with innovative and positive people and choose to think of them as an inspiration, as examples of the abundant goodness humans can discover and unleash. And, we can reach for our own positivity and goodness. Or we can choose denial of our own human potential, thus selecting the friction model of comparing our own negatives with their positives - in effect, comparing how we feel about ourselves with what they accomplish. In that case we will probably hear ourselves saying things like "I could never be like them - I mean they are great leaders, I am just me." We can then devalue ourselves by using abusive negative attention from belittling thoughts like "I'm weak, I'm a piece of sh#t, something has to be wrong with me to be like I am, I am totally worthless." These abrasive thoughts will create a negative outlook devoid of self-love and it is a comportment that most often brings us more of the same until we are lost in it. The results of this negative track can be seen in the folks suffering an enduring struggle without any sense of hope - without a connection to an internal light. At times this leads to giving up on life completely.

It is not easy to recognize that we have choices about

what and how we think, and where, when and how we pay attention to those thoughts, and how we express them. It is not easy to become accountable for our choices and therefore our perceptions and behaviors in this world. It is not easy. There can be momentous barriers undermining us at every turn along with discouragement from those around us. Sometimes owning this duty is harder than at other times. But it is still our own responsibility, no matter how challenging. If we are going to survive and thrive to live a healthy, happy and free life - it is incumbent on us to acknowledge and embrace that responsibility.

Some Affirmations for You

I pay attention to my thoughts and choose the ones I want to grow stronger.

I give attention to the things about myself that I want to grow.

I give myself encouraging thoughts.

I give myself love.

I pay attention to positive and loving thoughts I have for others.

I give myself respect.
I honor and respect the gift of life I have been given.

I choose to laugh at my negative, self-devaluing thoughts...They're just not true!

Suggested Exercise

You are invited to explore your attitude.

1) Describe your general daily attitude.

2) Describe your attitude when you are faced with arduous challenges.

3) Reread the quote by Viktor Frankl and describe what it means to you "to choose [your] own way."

Chapter Six

. . . .

THE VIRTUE OF LOVE

Love's greatest gift is its ability to make everything it touches sacred.

— Barbara de Angelis

There is no one definitive definition of love. It is something that we experience. I would venture to say that probably we humans all experience it in as many different ways as countless narratives, poems and songs have expressed it. Based on the narratives, poems and songs plus the various ways numerous people have described it, we can clearly see there are different kinds of love. And like happiness, love can run from shallow to the depths of our being.

To me, love is a gift of compassion, kindness, respect, trust, and generosity that is genuinely given and received with joy. Love is so big! It can heal small hurts and entire lives. It can bridge differences. It can mend minds and hearts. It is the love that nurtures happiness in our souls.

Love and Relationship Are Two Different Things

What is the difference? Well, love is described in the section above and relationship is the rapport between two or more individuals. Subsequently, I could say that relationship is how two people connect and love is what two people bring to the connection.

Here are two scenarios:

1) We get together and find we have a lot in common and then bond - but one or both of us brings baggage-unhealed emotional wounds, false beliefs, and unrealistic expectations instead of gifts of love

- and then the relationship bond gets stressed and possibly injured.

2) We have gifts of love that flow easily to one another; the chemistry is great yet one or both of us fails to understand the other, or we have opposing values - our love connection is full of static and eventually is disconnected. We need to have within us gifts of love and the capacity for relationship rapport to have a true-love relationship. The bad news is that most of us believe that love and relationship come to us automatically conjoined - and that is not always the case. The good news is that if we have love going for us, much of the time we can make adjustments in our relationship parts to create the compatibility necessary to culminate into a true-love story with a happy ending - or is it the beginning?

We are going to expand on the previous scenarios and explore some of the other assorted notions about love - some healthy and some unhealthy. We hopefully will see if and how any of the kinds of loves we look at mirror portions of our own relationships with ourselves and with others.

Romantic Love to True Love

In real love you want the other person's good. In romantic love you want the other person.

— Margaret Anderson

I remember being enthralled by the way love was portrayed in the movies. There were the great romantic models in films like *Casa Blanca, An Affair to Remember, Dr. Zhivago, The African Queen, Roman Holiday* - those romantic movies that they no longer make as often as they did in my younger years. They were the prototypes I tried to replicate in all my relationships over many years. Big mistake!

It was disappointing to learn that romance isn't the wherewithal of love; it's usually that physical attraction - that chemical jolt that brings two people together. Then the romantic pursuit is a lot of fun and stimulates all kinds of absorbing, intoxicating feelings. But without developing into something deeper, it usually evolves into something like a train wreck.

When I think about it, more often than not the recipients of my adoration, affection and romantic moves were not necessarily the recipients of my love! After more failures at relationships than I have room or desire to discuss here, I learned that, like most aspects of life, love is a matrix of essential qualities that combine to create a bond - the more numerous and stronger those essential qualities in the matrix are the stronger and more lasting the bond.

A healthy true-love relationship can grow out of an attraction when it is coupled with a sincere desire by each person for the other to be healthy, happy and free to be. This kind of love comes from the heart, with genuine, unadulterated good intentions. It is a gift that is to be given and received...flowing between partners. This flow creates trust and a base for equity in the relationship. Deep love-filled relationships are built on this stable foundation that provides a platform upon which aspects of both romance and true love - attraction, lovemaking, laughter, respect, communication, consideration, graciousness, and appreciation, etc. - can thrive.

Falling In "Love" -
A Step Toward Love Addiction?

> *When we're incomplete, we're always searching for somebody to complete us ... Nobody else can provide it for us, and to believe otherwise is to delude ourselves dangerously and to program for eventual failure every relationship we enter.*
>
> — Tom Robbins

Oh, I know this one. This is "madly in love" minus the essential qualities for healthy love. It is the experience of falling, falling into a breathless sweet pain where you can lose yourself...and sometimes it takes some time to find yourself again.

Often we addictive folks that are in recovery dance the lily-pod-hop, skipping from one addiction to another. During my early years in recovery from alcoholism, I shifted to love addiction.

It is a lonely-hearts' obsession - to find that special love. It is a roller-coaster ride full of thrills and torment. Those of us who carry around abandonment and/or intimacy issues baggage are very apt to develop love addiction.

You know when you are addicted to love because there is an intensity that sparks you and makes you feel alive and that is all you want. The respect, compassion, selflessness and trust that is part of a healthy love is secondary or lacking altogether. You can't go an hour without wanting to call and then obsessing bows to compulsion - and you call, you hear the voice on the other side, and relief washes over you. Time away from the person feels like dead time. When you are not with them then you are thinking about them. When you are with others you don't really want to talk about anything else but that person who is "the answer to your dreams." They excite you. You want them with you all the time - attached to your hip.

Then after a while they seem to be getting cool towards you - or you are feeling "smothered" by them; the excitement and intensity is dying down. Arguments begin to replace all the loving affection; the romantic passion is now found in the intensity of conflict. But you cannot stop thinking about that person and calling them five, ten, even more times a day. They pull away and you pursue them. Then the break-up comes and with that, more calls...then distance and silence...then they call you or you call them and you accept each other's apologies and seductive attitudes...and it starts all over again. And that cycle continues until someone else comes along that gives you that same excitement and intensity and makes you feel so loved.

You know this time it is different...then it goes through the same cycle. So it goes until you reach out for help from a therapist that specializes in love addiction or get into the appropriate Twelve Step Program...hopefully both!

Love Addict: Sex, Romance, and Other Dangerous Drugs

Just because something is addictive doesn't mean
that you will get addicted to it.
But...if your stomach ties up in knots while
you count the seconds waiting for a phone call
from that special someone...
if you hear a loud buzzing in your ears
when you see a certain person's car
(or one just like it)... if your eyes burn when you
hear a random love song or see a couple holding
hands.... if you suffer the twin agonies of craving
for and withdrawing from a series of
unrequited crushes or toxic relationships...
if you always feel like you're clutching
at someone's ankle and dragged
across the floor as they try to leave the room...
welcome to the club.

—Ethlie Ann Vare,
Love Addict, Sex, Romance, and Other Dangerous Drugs

Let us remember that in a healthy, true-love relationship we are attentive to what we want to "give" to the other person and in an unhealthy addictive-type relationship we will be fixated on what we ourselves "want" to get or think we "need" to get and "how" 'we are going to get it. When both of us in a liaison are capable of participating in a wholesome, true-love relationship then both of us will be wanting to "give" to the other which leads to a flowing exchange of caring; if one of us is not able to sustain participation in a true-love relationship we will send messages that the other never gives "enough" or "right-enough."

If we are basically emotionally stable we will not have tolerance for this behavior and will let go of what we consider an unhealthy relationship. And if we are both unable to participate consistently in a true-love relationship we will throw the never gives "right-enough" complaints at each other until that sick, cyclical game of "come here-go away" becomes the core of the relationship, which then lasts until one of us gets tired of playing and throws in the towel.

What I did:

I reached out for help and broke the cycle.

After exploring a variety of definitions for love, I wrote a list of mutually given attributes that I believe are contributors to healthy love. They are: Respect, Compassion, Affection, Attention, Trust, Consideration, Thoughtfulness, Appreciation, Allowance, and Acceptance.

I began to explore what I wanted to give to others to show my own love. I picked a former unrequited love and wrote a letter that I did NOT send, allowing myself to write about my love without any expectation for it to be returned. Through this exercise I got in touch with some of the love inside me that was there to give freely. Then I wrote a letter of acceptance and gratitude to this love within me. Then I took that not-sent letter and burned it, releasing my love to the Universe through the smoke...I looked at myself in the mirror each day and told myself, "I love you."...The letter to the love within me I kept to reread now and again to remind me that this love is there and is growing!

I practiced using three of the virtues - acceptance, gratitude, constructive attention - within all my relationships-including the one with myself. I began a routine of consciously paying constructive attention and accepting compliments and acts of kindness. I created a Relationship Gratitude Box where I deposited written notes expressing my gratitude for thoughtful acts from my friends and family members. As I practiced all these things I became more conscious and formed healthier and healthier relationships in every area of my life.

Suggested Exercise

You are invited to explore.

Johann Wolfgang von Goethe said;
"Love does not dominate; it cultivates."

What does this mean to you?

The Web of Life...Universal Love

And while I stood there I saw more than I can tell and I understood more than I saw; for I was seeing in a sacred manner the shapes of things in the spirit, and the shape of all shapes as they must live together like one being.

— Black Elk
(from the book *Black Elk Speaks*)

In the last couple of decades I came to see that this description by Black Elk illustrates the kind of love that I have been most involved in growing in my life, because I can give and receive the most joy and satisfaction through it. It is the kind of love that I can find anywhere and everywhere. I experience it with all that lives in the Sky - clouds, stars, planets, moon and sun; all that lives on the Earth: mountains, deserts, and valleys - the stones, the two-legged, the four-legged, the winged ones, the water beings, the trees and all that grows green. I feel it in the wind; in the fire; in the water. It is flowing in and out and through all of life. It is the love that I fill myself with and give away daily. It flows through me and I become love in motion...Like a tree responding to a breeze; like the sun's gentle beam kissing the mountain peaks good morning and good night; like the river shaping and polishing the Earth as it cuts its path through it; like the glistening stones' welcoming song to the river always arriving. Oh, the flow of love through it all!

To be connected with life is to not feel superior or inferior; it is about knowing your part in the web. As I have learned, our part is to be stewards of life on Earth. If you are going to do that well, it is a good idea to be in communion with life...to love it... for that which we love, truly love, we protect and care for to the best of our ability. And we understand without explanation, and accept without understanding; and trust without stipulation. I know this connection with life.

Each day I look here
and there and everywhere
Captivated by its endless beauty and grace
As it softly sings its sweet songs
And performs its dazzling dances
My heart gives itself unto the free-flowing web
As it fulfills me like no other love ever has

Sometime in the mid-nineteen-nineties I was invited to an American Indian Medicine Wheel Ceremony, which teaches many things; one being the interconnections between all parts of life...the seen and unseen. The Wheel Ceremony was hosted and guided by Dr. Janice Kalec. The initial significant awareness for me was that the Wheel is built with stones and one of my first teachings was to recognize that stones are alive...that they have energy that is transmittable. I accepted this possibility. My ability to be accepting had grown pretty strong by that time. So as far as I could see, accepting the possibility that all the Creator's creations, including stones, are alive wouldn't hurt anyone - so why not? I even liked the idea! Deep in my gut I felt that it was a natural truth that I cannot explain. It just is.

Janice and I became friends. Over the years that connection, like my connection to all my relations, has grown deep. I am also very grateful to my Kola (friend in Lakota). She taught me how to gather stones for the Medicine Wheel. We walked along the dry river beds and there I learned to listen for the stones to call me. I would find myself turning my head and looking directly at a stone maybe ten feet away and I would go to it and pick it up and feel its energy and I'd "know" it wanted to come with me. So I'd bag it and leave a pinch of natural tobacco or cornmeal in the place that held it, with a prayer of "thank you." Sometimes I'd be attracted to a stone, pick it up, and "know" that although it was interesting, it was not interested and did not want to leave its spot - and so I returned it.

I went to many, many Medicine Wheel Ceremonies. The Wheel resonated with me and I with it, and another new world opened up to me. I reconnected with my indigenous roots in this land we call America. I came to know a community built on mutual respect, honor and heartfelt caring for all its relations - I came to know a world consisting of an intricate web of magnificent connections that included all that the Creator created; my eyes and heart opened.

I saw a cycle of life that offered an abundance of the really important things - the stuff that can't be bought: love, relatedness, respect, courage, guidance, nurturing, healing, joy, challenges, and fulfillment of the senses. I grew to honor ALL life!

I began to grasp some of the ways of my Tongva lineage. I learned that my greatest teachers are animals, trees, stones, water and air. As I started to pay more attention to what I call "my relations," I began to understand life better and grew to believe that everything has an intelligence and purpose that affects everything else. I noticed that the more I paid attention to the life around me the closer I felt to it. My connection with all my relations expanded and I learned to pay attention to our interactions. Following is a story of one of those relationships...

Some years back, I was driving north on Highway 14 in California. I had my car filled with camping gear for 7-9 women. I was guiding a handful of women who were joining me on a camping retreat that would be about connecting to life. I had a friend who was riding shotgun with me. The other women were following us in two other cars. As we were driving along, just before we got to the Interstate 395 junction, my friend asked, "By the way where are we going?"... "I don't know," I answered...."What? You don't know! But...but you have these women following you...and you don't know where you are taking them?" she exclaimed. "It is okay," I said and continued, "Don't worry. We will be taken to exactly where we are supposed to be." She took a breath or two and said, "Alright...you've always seemed to know." I explained to her, to the best of my ability, that I trusted something deep inside; I had this feeling I was choosing to follow. I did know we were going to be around the Mammoth area. I just didn't know exactly where. And I reassured her that it was going to be the perfect place for us.

We had been traveling for a while on I-395; we arrived in Bishop, stopped and had some lunch. My friend did not say a word about not having a campground reserved. I smiled at that, interpreting that as her trust in the unfolding of the journey. It was late afternoon and we had driven through Lone Pine where I took a little detour to Manzanar Memorial - a ritual of mine. We all smudged (cleansed with sage). I asked everyone to find a place that they were drawn to and offer a prayer for peace, for the souls that has passed through there, and for those that lingered. I gave an offering of tobacco and we were silent for a period. Then we returned to our vehicles and were off again to our "secret" destination.

About 10 miles south of Tom's Place on Rock Creek, a crow dipped from the heavens and began to fly along the highway in front of us, leading us. I glanced at my friend and she was looking at me with "I'll be damned" written all over her smiling face! I said, "We are going to follow her to our camping place...as the crow flies, so will we." And so it was. Our crow-guide turned into the road to Tom's Place, passed Tom's and went on toward Rock Creek campgrounds. Then she took a turn to the left and following her we descended into a beautiful group campground, surrounded by tall pines and set back from the banks of Rock Creek. I parked and the crow circled us. I waved at her and hollered, "Perfect! Thank you!" and she disappeared through the pines. I stretched, then smiled as I looked up the sheer cliff, reaching from the camping area to the road above...and on it I saw nature's etching of a spread-winged eagle! I knew we were in the right place. I told the women that we had arrived and to unpack and set-up camp. I went to the camp office and was informed that there was no reservation on the group camp area and that it was all ours. We spent four lovely days there, connecting to all of our relations!

Suggested Exercise

Write a poem, a story or a description depicting your relationship or a special moment with nature.

Healing Power of Love

The cure for all the ills and wrongs, the cares, the sorrows, and the crimes of humanity, all lie in the one word "love." It is the divine vitality that everywhere produces and restores life.

—Lydia M. Child

Life is Spirit, an energy flow. To remove your Self from even part of the flow is to disconnect from part of life - and this dilutes love, inviting affliction. Therefore, I am proposing that if we are solidly connected to the flow of life, love will be strong and so will our resistance to afflictions. I personally agree with the many that proclaim love to be healing.

Have you ever felt the relaxing, comforting quality of warm hands on your shoulders, back, neck or head? I have. Headaches have dissipated with healing strokes to my brow. My aching knees have had their throbbing melted away by a gentle touch streaming love. When we have loving thoughts our energy is infused with love and that love moves through our bodies and can be shared with others.

The energy of love is miraculous.

Sometime in the spring of 1987, I was lying in a Long Beach, California hospital bed, recovering from an emergency life-saving surgery, when a nurse came into my room, stood at the foot of the bed and informed me that I had cervical cancer and needed to see my gynecologist as soon as I was back on my feet from this surgery. I was a bit stunned, then thought, "I don't think that's true and there's nothing I can do about it right now." So I shook it off and didn't think about it until I was discharged. Then I told a therapist friend (whom I will refer to as "J"), who had been through something similar. J had used Dr. O. Carl Simonton's body-mind approach to address her cancer and it had worked for her. I liked that idea. But as yet I had not seen the gynecologist and was going to wait to make sure that I had "something" to deal with for sure. It took 2-3 weeks for me to recuperate enough to get to the gynecologist. She examined me and took a piece of my cervix to biopsy. I left there feeling sure that I was okay. Three days later I received a call to return to the office the next day. I did and was informed that the biopsy was positive and that another test needed to be completed the following week to determine the best avenue of treatment. I felt a little confused but I was not stressed, or distressed; I left there again, feeling sure that I was okay. I sat in my car for what I think was 10 minutes...contemplating and meditating. I accepted that the gynecologist had discovered cancer cells. I accepted that in my heart of hearts I knew there was nothing to be concerned about. I decided that, even though I was sure I was going to be fine, I would follow the doctor's directions and I would also follow the way conveyed to me by the soft voice from deep inside me...what I call my Soul Whisperer.

When I got home I called the gynecologist's office and made an appointment for the following week. Then I called J. I told her what the doctor had determined and explained that "I knew" (from my Soul Whisperer) I was to begin some mind-body work before I saw the doctor again. She was very supportive and we made a date to meet at her office in Westlake Village in a couple of days.

During my meeting with J she taught me how to use self-hypnosis to go into deep relaxation. We discussed the need for me to create an imagery that fit my needs. I was listening closely to the quiet voice and my choice was to use an aggressive imagery. And I shared with J that I had already seen the imagery.

It was as follows...

There were black shriveled cells scattered around my cervix. I could see them all. I raked them into a pile. As I raked them, I thanked them for all the good work they had done and now it was time for them to be taken away. Then in my head I called for two black Dobermans, "Come. Now." They came running at full speed and delved into the pile of shriveled black cells, devouring them and then running back to wherever they came from. Then I took a breath and told all the healthy plump cells in my cervix that I loved them and was very grateful for them and that I would pay attention to keeping them healthy and strong. I could feel the energy moving throughout my lower abdomen as I sent love to my entire cervix and all my female organs.

After I shared the image with J, she said it was a strong image and I should see it in my mind as often as I could each day. That is what I did. The quiet soft voice inside me - I call my "Soul Whisperer" - reassured me that I was fine and I did not experience any stress or worry. I imagined the black shriveled cells, raking them into a pile, the Doberman's devouring them and running off, countless times a day. At least three times a day I'd practice self-hypnosis, going into a deeply relaxed state, and when I came out of that profoundly serene place, I'd tell myself, "I love you." I'd feel strong and healthy. And at times a tear or two of joy trickled down my cheek.

It seemed like I'd been doing this routine for weeks and it had only been days before I was back to the doctors. Again, I was on the examining table, feet in the stirrups, and another piece of my cervix was cut from me for additional tests. The doctor explained to me that she would confer with her colleagues regarding the results of the test and then let me know if treatment was going to be freezing, medications, or surgery. I said thank you, left there, and resumed my deep relaxation-imagery routine.

I got a call from the doctor's office a few days later and was asked to come into the office the next day. I did. As usual I was put into an examining room. The doctor entered. She looked at me with a puzzled expression and said, "I cannot believe it. Your cells came back from this last test looking healthy. It seems impossible but now your test is negative for cervical cancer." I asked, "Are you sure?" "Yes" she responded. You do not show any signs of cancer in your cervix." I said, "Thank you," smiled, left that office and never returned, understanding the healing power of love.

Suggested Exercise

Sit somewhere comfortable. Take a couple of relaxing breaths. Close your eyes and imagine loving energy flowing from your heart and throughout your body; then focus on the energy flowing through your arms into your hands. Now begin to let your hand touch one another...feel the love flowing and then put your hands on your face, chest, and wherever you feel the desire to be touched. When you are finished, bring your right hand to your heart and then cover with your left hand. Breathe gently and open your eyes...enjoy the love!

Is there a part of yourself that you want to strengthen or encourage to be healthier? If so, you may want to write imagery here just for you.

Remember to put in the Love.

Authentic Self-Love Is Unconditional

> *You can search throughout the entire universe for someone who is more deserving of your love and affection than you are yourself, and that person is not to be found anywhere. You yourself, as much as anybody in the entire universe, deserves your love and affection.*
>
> — Buddha

This love is the source from which we nurture all our other love. It is the love of our Soul.

I remember the time when I was afraid to look inside myself because I thought I'd discover that I was empty or evil - completely devoid of love. When I finally sucked it up and took a look - paradoxically, I discovered that I had tons of love inside me waiting to be expressed. I just didn't know how to give it. More than a few people suggested to me that I had to learn to give love to myself before I could genuinely give it to others. I thought that was corny but I was willing to try anything to fill that empty hole in the pit of my stomach. This is not about narcissistic love. Remember, Narcissus fell in love with his reflection in a pond which he could not leave without leaving his greatest love - his image - and needless to say, he starved to death. What I am suggesting is that you love your Soul - your Authentic Self, your Total Being! Who you are is not your appearance, not your image! This kind of love, full of self-acceptance, self-respect, self-care, self-reliance, self-accord, and self-appreciation for your true self, the living Soul your Creator made you to be - this love sets you free instead of entrapping you. It nurtures your Soul versus starving you. Big difference!

To love our Soul absolutely is to love our Great Spirit - which some call God, the Source, the Universe, the Higher Power...Whatever you call it...It is unrestricted love that creates an everlasting eternal spring of unconditional love from which we nurture all our other genuine loves. It is our source for healing energy. It is this authentic love within us that reflects goodness in all that we see. It is this love that connects all of us in the web of life in a "good" way. It is our vital love. When it is released it flows to and from all life. We give it freely, without conditions or expectations, for it will not be given in any other way. And in the same unrestricted way it returns to us!

Here is a list of some things I did:

Looked in the mirror and said, "I love you" - with feeling! (I experimented with several tones and expressions. Have some fun with it.)

Performed simple acts of kindness, like giving a smile; a hug.

Kept a small notebook and listed actions that I completed which produced a loving feeling within me.

Made a list of all of my positive qualities and read them daily.

Once a week, I did something "special" for me such as: took a long bubble bath, got a massage, had a movie marathon day, took a day drive with no destination just to explore, or stayed in my PJ's all day and read.

Once a week, for 12 weeks, I did something nice for someone else without announcing what I did (I kept it between myself and the Great Spirit) - like sending a greeting card sans signature, taking a neighbor's paper up to their porch, picking up trash on the beach, sending anonymous donations, sending someone who is struggling financially a grocery store or gas gift card.

I practiced generosity with all my assets - time, skills, abilities, attention, and money.

Once a month I wrote my Self a letter validating all that I liked about me and thanking me for all that I'd done to help my progress on my life's journey.

Suggested Exercise

You are invited to do any or all of the things I did plus the following:

Write or draw your dreams for yourself ... for all that you love.

Repeat the Self-Acceptance affirmations in the Virtue of Acceptance Chapter.

Give yourself love and compassion for 5-10 minutes a day.

Put yourself in a safe, quiet comfortable place, sit or lay down and take deep slow breaths. Wrapping your arms around yourself, say the following:

"I am safe; I am loved just as I am; I am healthy; I am peaceful."

Repeat these thoughts over to yourself for at least 5 minutes; allow yourself to add any other good thoughts about you. Then send these compassionate thoughts to others. Be conscious that someone is most likely sending you positive thoughts so open-up your heart and receive them!

If you choose, write a description of your experience.

Suggested Exercise

Paint a picture, make a collage, write a poem, a short story, or simply make a list that describes your Authentic Self as you know it today. The Authentic Self changes like everything else! After all it does grow with nurturing and shrink with neglect. There is no right or wrong way of doing this...just play and enjoy!

Here's a place just for you to make a list of things you could do to grow your unconditional love for your Self.

Chapter Seven

. . . .

SPIRIT AND ITS RELATIONSHIP WITH THE FOUR VIRTUES?

Ride the energy of your own unique spirit

— Gabrielle Roth

I believe Spirit is our flow of energy - the energy flow that creates a vibration that telegraphs our nature out into the world. It is sometimes referred to as our personality.

I have come to a deduction that some of us are blessed with a primarily calm flow of energy; some of us are blessed with a predominantly intense energy flow; and most of us are blessed with an energy flow vibration that mainly lies between calm and intense. Generally, our energy moves along the spectrum of calm to intense. I envision Spirit as the stuff that synchronizes life transformations. How Spirit goes forth defines how we are seen and experienced - from stoic to exuberant.

Spirit is the vibrational thread that designs the interconnected relationships between all things that exist. How we relate is determined by what our energy's vibrational flow consists of - for that affects our thoughts and is affected by our thoughts - which together influence our state of being. Our Spirit - Energy flow -transmits what our energy consists of - positive or negative or both - into and back from our environment. If our Spirit is comprised of positive thoughts that inspire and are inspired by acceptance, gratitude, constructive attention and love, that is what it will project out into the world and that is what it will attract from others. That positive energy from others then flows back into our Spirit and then Spirit absorbs it and delivers it to our inner workings - thoughts and feelings and physical conditions. However, if our Spirit consists of negative characteristics like judgment, criticism, thanklessness, and indifference then that is what we will attract. And that is what Spirit will transport back into our inner world. So, as I see it, Spirit is a dynamic energy source with a vibrational delivery service.

There are those special cases where our Spirit is blocked by barriers, usually caused by false beliefs that will not allow it to flow. This is when our personality is not emerging from our essence - our authentic self - but is instead a façade we built to keep us safe. We sometimes believe we cannot allow the natural flow of Spirit - Energy - Life Force to go out because we will become diminished, or come in because we will be hurt. In these cases we need to focus on understanding Spirit and how to engage it to help build a true sense of Self - to discover who we truly are. Otherwise we can go through life feeling "phony" or "isolated" - or "wronged," which can result in feeling we are not connected to anything that gives us a sense of "belonging."

Conducting Our Energy

Spirit is not a mystic concept.
The spirit of a person is manifest in her aliveness, brightness of his eyes, in the resonance of her voice and in the ease and gracefulness of movements. These qualities are related to and stem from a high level of energy in the body... Sensing the harmony between the internal pulsation of our body and that in the universe, we feel identified with the universal, with God. We are like tuning forks vibrating at the same pitch.

— Alexander Lowen

It was as a client in a couple's therapy session that I learned about the flow of energy between people. During this time my energy could spontaneously grow so big it bowled others over. I was told that my partner sometimes experienced me like a powerful tidal wave, giving her no room to express herself! My partner's energy, on the other hand, moved like a subtle, languid breeze that I didn't experience at all, or could only experience very faintly.

My partner explained that during our interactions I often came across so loud and strong that she didn't know how to communicate with me. She could hardly get a word interjected so she just listened and then turned me off at some point. So then I shared that my experience with her was that she didn't have much to say and I always had to carry our conversations!

The therapist explained that we each had to make an adjustment for the other. She suggested that I needed to be aware of coming on strong and hold myself back a little. She suggested that my partner seemed to be passing the responsibility for our interactions onto me and that she could explore this. Then she suggested that my partner get a little bigger and step up and assert herself a bit more.

I analyzed this information for a time. I considered my use of my energy at different times, under different conditions, and came to the conclusion that if I became more conscious of my energy, I could conduct it like a symphony. I could change the melody of my expressions.

I began to sing in an opera-like style in the shower, altering my volume. In conversations I slowed my speech. I read aloud, fluctuating my tone and volume. Okay! - I learned I could consciously change my oral presentation to create a mood....Then I sat at the seashore and listened to the waves. I noticed the difference between the power of a large wave crashing on the shore and a small wave caressing the shore. I listened to the wind and heard the difference between a breeze and a windstorm. As I listened to the waves and the wind, I paid attention to how I experienced them. The soft waves and gentle winds had a calming, nurturing effect on me. The big waves and the windstorms had an exciting, intensifying effect on me. With these experiences, I recognized how my movements and verbal communications could affect those around me. So there it was, I could affect, even create, an atmosphere consciously. Unconsciously, I had been doing this in my professional work for years...you know, that "therapist's voice." Yep. It is creating a gentle wave and breeze in the room...a caring, nurturing, safe place. Can you imagine what a therapist I would have been coming across like a windstorm?

This is simply a way of shaping the use of our energy!

Oh! The partner relationship did not survive. However, I am forever grateful to that therapist because I changed a lot in my life with this information. My awareness and sensing ability has been significantly heightened. I am much more conscious in my interactions, and know I improved them four-fold. The flow of my Spirit has become more diverse, allowing me to be more of who I am.

Now I often explain to clients that they are the conductors of their energy, presenting a symphony through their expressions. They can present themselves using a range from decrescendo to crescendo and from crescendo to decrescendo. What is important is to know their audience and what they want to express. After all, the energy force - Spirit - is the wave, the wind upon which they flow out into their space, their domain, their world, their universe.

Ways You Can Get in Touch with Your Energy...Spirit

> *Energetics" is a word I coined to speak about the unseen energies of life - the invisible vibrations that flow in, around, and between each of us and everything in our universe; vibrations that though unseen, affect us and are affected by us.*
>
> — Elaine Seiler

You can visit the seashore and listen to the waves or listen to the winds like I did.

You can watch and listen to a river.

You can listen to a symphony!

Play on a drum...expressing your feelings, like sadness, anger, loneliness, happiness, and fear.

Suggested Exercise

Following is a simple positive energy flow exercise I do:

Stand tall, turn your face upward and stretch your arms out toward the sky, slightly cupping your hands as if you are going to catch a beach ball. Now let your hands fill with energy from the universe. When you feel the energy in your hands beginning to tingle, focus on it. Hold on to it for 10-30 seconds, feeling its warmth and love. Then feel it move up your arms into the trunk of your body, down into your lower abdomen, then up into your chest, feeling your heart slowly filling with the warm, loving energy. Then slowly lower your arms, placing your palms facing down, sharing the energy with the Earth. Take a deep breath. Relax. Enjoy your day and - I hope you try this...it is great!

Other ways to get your energy flowing:

Take a walk, staying conscious of the feeling of the earth beneath your feet.

Go outdoors and let the breeze caress your skin. Feel its energy entering your pores. Soak it in. You can also do this with the sun.

Sing or chant, play with the notes using your body like a scale; feel the sounds vibrate through your chakras.

Sit near water and listen until you can feel the sound.

Can you think of other ways that you get your energy flowing? You can list them here...

Awaking to Spirit

As I progressed in my spiritual growth, I began to spend more quiet time with myself. I began to meditate more effectively - and I awakened to my inner world. A light was ignited within me that has continued to shine. With that Spark of Life came a connection to my energy - an energy that I have learned to use to heal; to grow strong; to enhance my love; to nurture clarity and wisdom. When Spirit bolstered me into a state of communion with my Soul - my Authentic-Self, I came to understand what being whole means.

Indications that we are connected and whole are when...

We accept and love who we are and how we are in relationship to all we know - we see that we are unique, constantly changing, growing, evolving Authentic Selves, and yet we remain a part of a web that likewise persistently evolves.

We are compelled to grow - naturally expanding our minds and hearts, and learning experiences throughout our lives.

We can hear that quiet voice inside and follow it... even when a part of us is saying, "That's nuts."

We are aware of choosing to be motivated and directed by our Spirit.

We are flexible and can adapt to changes around us - the changes in the web of life - without completely losing our balance.

We take the responsibility to nurture our Spirit with Acceptance, Gratitude, Constructive Attention and Love and all of our other positive thoughts and feelings. And we then become aware that our Spirit will deliver these virtues through us out into the world.

> *The spiritual path - is simply the journey of living our lives. Everyone is on a spiritual path; most people just don't know it."*
>
> — Marianne Williamson

Suggested Exercise

You are invited to sit quietly with your Spirit moving within you and around you, as you talk with it, telling all that it means to you. If you like, when you are done, you can write or draw or doodle your experience right here.

Spirit is Playful...Lighten-Up!

Things I have done that I invite you to try in the shower:

Sing opera in the shower...and in the middle of an argument, break out into an operatic delivery of your point of view.

Buy your favorite ice cream and some cones. Prepare to take a shower. Put on a robe and make yourself an ice cream cone. Take it into the shower where you can eat without worry about making a mess. Let it melt down your arms. Taste its cold softness, feel it melt on your lips, your tongue, down your body's front side; feel the hot shower pouring over your body; feel the contrast of the cold and hot. It's crazy! It's silly! Enjoy!

Eat a slice of ice cold watermelon while taking a hot bath - that is great fun, too.

Write graffiti messages or draw funny pictures on the steam-fogged shower doors.

Buy some Jacks or Pick-up Sticks and play...it's great on a rainy day.

Read your favorite children's book aloud to yourself.

Pick up a coloring book and crayons and COLOR!

Things I Invite you to do Outdoors:

While hiking, when you come across a level stretch, stop walking and start skipping! It's fun! (Thank you, Bibi Caspari, for reminding me about the power of skipping.)

Smile at every person you see on a walk.

Stop and lay on your back in the park or yard and look for shapes in the clouds.

Actually hug a tree. Try it ... Check out whether you can feel its energy coming into you. Tree Huggers are cool people!

Find a labyrinth in your vicinity and walk it.

Watch a squirrel, a crow or another bird, or a rabbit until it is out of sight. Let it entertain you until it is gone.

> *We don't stop playing because we grow old; we grow old because we stop playing.*
>
> — George Bernard Shaw

Just for fun:

Wear a top inside out or backwards and see if anyone tells you.

Use crayons and draw a funny self-portrait on a sheet of paper.

Fix your dinner and try eating it with other utensils you find in your kitchen instead of flatware.

Buy an inexpensive harmonica or recorder and play the silliest song that you know.

Make a funny greeting card for someone you think could use it. And give it to them.

Laugh for no reason...just laugh all kinds of different laughs...try them on! If you need a reason, make funny faces in a mirror. Laugh...a lot! Lighten up!

Just do something silly now and again!

Spirit and The Power of Belief

> *Each one of us has our own evolution of life, and each one of us goes through different tests which are unique and challenging. But certain things are common. And we do learn things from each other's experience. On a spiritual journey, we all have the same destination.*
>
> — A. R. Rahman

Power of Belief...Believing in possibilities creates a difference. If I had not believed that change was possible, I would not have incorporated acceptance, gratitude, constructive attention, and love into my live...and I would not know Authentic Intrinsic Happiness. If it were not for my faith in my Essence, in the Great Mystery and in the unstoppable unfolding of Life, I would not have ever experienced the life force of Spirit sending my message of happiness out into the world through my changed nature. I would not have experienced my hero's journeys...big and small; long and short...all challenging.

> *In the confrontation between the stream and the rock, the stream always wins - not through strength, but through persistence.*
>
> — Buddha

The Story of Little Stream

There once was a long line of bending water called Little Stream. It wasn't sure where it came from but it thought it was from somewhere far away and high. It had been running along the same ol' way for a long, long time, longer that it could remember. And it verily remembered that occasion long ago when a great bolt of light came out of the sky and splintered a Sycamore with more branches than hair on a dog and then slammed the tree down - right across its own streaming path. For a while it was able to get through the branches. Then as pieces and bits of other debris caught on the tree, Little Stream was able to eke a tiny bit of its self through. The rains stopped coming. Then the rocks and mud and other debris gathered in the Sycamore branches and created a wall that dammed up Little Stream's flow. Where the flow was stuck a small pond was born. At first it was kind of pretty. Then it began to turn ugly... a foul yellow-green, slimy moss began to form on it until it was mucky and dark. The birds wouldn't play in it. The coyotes wouldn't drink from it. Even the frogs were starting to move out. It grew so stagnant that the only things hanging around were the mosquitoes.

Since the rains and melting snow were growing more and more scarce, Little Stream just couldn't get enough power built up to get into motion and clean itself. It certainly couldn't muster up the strength to free itself. All it could manage was to every now and again trickle a sip or two over its barrier. Very slowly it made a thin, wimpy showing that leaked into a marsh. Little Stream felt its life going out and knew it would soon be lost if it wasn't set free to be all that it could be. The sun's rays were like straws draining it. But Little Stream still did not lose hope. If it couldn't do anything else, it could dream, pray and keep moving the best it could.

Every time sprinkles fell from the sky, no matter how lightly, Little Stream was grateful and focused on every drop that was added to it and every movement that made it feel stronger. Now Little Stream communed with its Maker and gave thanks for the many years of joy there had been in its gentle, steady flow, passing the Scrub Oaks and Sycamores and washing over stones large and small. It had been a strong running stream, splashing over stones, plunging down angles, growing into a river, until this dry spell came. Now it accepted its situation and looked around with love for the life left in it and on its banks. Little Stream just kept crawling around and around the big and little rocks and kept slipping wearily over the pebbles, waiting for the times to change, believing with every drop of its being that it would flow fast and steady again.

Then it happened-it began to sprinkle...and sprinkle... and sprinkle. Then it rained. Then it rained and rained and rained. The sky growled and great bolts of light came shooting down, striking the banks....... and then one bolt hit the fallen sycamore and cracked the dam! Little Stream was free! It flowed! It grew and it grew! It swelled larger than it had ever been! Little Stream now felt strong and vital! It was so grateful! It loved its flow! It loved the banks it was rising up against! Little Stream became what it was meant to be-a River that meandered for miles, supplying irrigation for crops and cattle, for sheep and horses to have cool drinks and splish-splash baths, as it followed its course to the sea where it would lose itself, only to be found again.

Today, The River, once called Little Stream, glistens and dances with happiness that it shares with its every turn, gurgling with glee as it energetically churns its way along its joyful journey.

Discovered in a Dream

The first peace, which is the most important, is that which comes within the souls of people when they realize their relationship, their oneness with the universe and all its powers, and when they realize that at the center of the universe dwells the Great Spirit and that its center is really everywhere, it is within each of us.

— Black Elk, *The Road Home*

An authentic happiness born from a true heart is not easy to come by; I walked around without it for longer than I expected; of course, not many of my intentions have ever unfolded as I planned .... I had counted on luck or a reward at the end of a maze.

Now I don't believe I could ever find it through luck, or as a reward. I believe it is found in Dorothy's dream - your dream and my dream at the end of the rainbow. And the only way to get there is through the Land of Oz, taking that chilling jaunt filled with witches, flying monkeys and false wizards who conjure up boundless misfortunes to challenge us as we try to get it. On my way I may search out wise counsel. Then I ask, "What is wise? What is wicked?" It is hard to tell on the scary road. So, "Get off the road," I order myself, "Rest in the field of poppies. Fall into a deep sleep," I urge.

I do, losing myself within my reveries. Wherein I see a tree teeming with strange fruit, shaped like apples, pears, bananas, and mangos. And then I see what seems so strange about them: the fruits are labelled, not with "Organic," but with "Acceptance," "Gratitude," "Constructive Attention," and "Love." On the trunk of the tree are letters arranged vertically spelling out "Spirit."

I eat and eat until I am sated. I hear the birds' songs, the leaves chatting, and the roots of the trees growing. I enter into a peaceful rest.....And after a while my eyes open. I am awake and see anew - then comes a realization that I am on the road home and am a happy peaceful Soul flowing free, connected to You, Me and Everything.

CONCLUSION

Be the change you want to see in the world.

— Mahatma Gandhi

I have shared some of what I value most about me - my experiences, practices and insights related to the four virtues of acceptance, gratitude, constructive attention and love plus their relationship to spirit - energy. I have shown you how from the depths of my misery I evolved into a truly happy human being. It is my hope that From Misery To Happiness provides you with a way - by practicing one or more of these virtues -- to an intrinsic, genuine happiness of your own. It is simple. It is challenging. But, with conscious effort and a strong desire you can do it - if I could anyone can. You choose your path, your journey to happiness; it doesn't happen to you from "out there." It is an "inside job" of self-discovery and dedicated practice of virtues that are change agents. I am confident that if you want authentic happiness you will create it, if not through the methods that worked for me, then through another way. To have happiness you must be a humane, grateful and loving person - it doesn't matter how you grow these traits within you - just do it!

My Closing Sermon...

> *I alone cannot change the world, but I can cast a stone across the waters to create many ripples.*
>
> — Mother Teresa

Our families, our communities and our world need more support and healing. As I see it, the responsible thing to do is to be part of the change. So let's continue to make positive changes and grow - and through our example inspire our families and friends to do the same. It is a journey of "attraction, not promotion."

We can be part of the solution and change the tide of greed, hate and violence in our communities. I invite you to join me in a campaign to spread the virtues of happiness...acceptance, gratitude, constructive attention, and love...And see the alchemy of loving goodness transform: repugnance into acceptance, discontent into gratitude, disparaging attention into constructive attention, cruelty into love, and an economic-centered world into a Spirit-centered one.

Then we shall have proactive cooperation where there is now reactive competition. We shall have peace where there is conflict. We shall have abundance where there is lack. We shall have health where there is sickness. We shall have learning where there is ignorance. We shall awaken from our nightmares and enter our dreams. Now some - probably more like a lot - call this "Pollyanna," or idealistic. Yes. How did having an idealistic view get to be judged and condemned as pointless, ridiculous or impossible? Perhaps this is the underlying "problem" creating continual clashes around the planet. Somehow we have agreed to settle for a mundane, uninvolved existence that espouses mediocre expectations and cynicism that seems to encourage a dominate-subordinate paradigm. This pattern doesn't create happiness or places where happiness can survive, let alone thrive.

So I suggest wholeheartedly that we each raise the bar on our expectations of ourselves. Let's expect ourselves to do better and be better - expect ourselves to expand and evolve - to be better at accepting, to be in gratitude more often, more consistently, to grow more unconditional love, to grow love deeper and more meaningfully in our life, to give our attention more constructively, and to take economics out of the driver's seat of our life and make it become a slice of it instead - and let's put Spirit back in its rightful place in the center of our life - in the driver's seat. If we do strive for this profound progress, we will give our life much greater meaning and know authentic happiness - and then spread it through our own attitude wherever we are. May we meet again on the road to a happy, fulfilling destiny.

A New Beginning....

Go Shining - You are the star of your life!

Notes

Notes

Notes

ABOUT THE AUTHOR

Carolyn Berry, MA, LMFT, a native Californian, has spent nearly 40 years helping people to emotionally heal and to reach for their human potential. In this role, she has worked as a Life Coach, a Marriage Family Therapist and an Addictions Counselor.

Carolyn became interested in "being happy" as a teenager and strived to find happiness during the first half of her adult life. It was in her late 60's that the author realized that she was truly happy most of the time, and at the age of 70, she decided to backtrack to map out how she had grown happiness in her life.

From Misery to Happiness is the result of two years of exploring what she had learned. The book looks at the life practices Carolyn adopted that led this wise woman to becoming the authentically happy person she continues to be to the present day. Today, she resides in Abiquiu, New Mexico, where she enjoys life along the Chama River.

www.carolynberry.com

39148243R00108

Made in the USA
Middletown, DE
16 March 2019